LET'S PUT SOME LIPSTICK ON THIS PIG?

Innovative Insights and Practical Applications for the Selling Professional

MARK MCGLINCHEY

Business Management Solutions
Indianapolis, Indiana

Business Management Solutions
Indianapolis, Indiana
www.mcglincheygroup.com

ISBN 0-9728076-0-8

Edited by Cynthia D. McMillan
Cover Design by Communique
Interior and Text Design by April Altman Reynolds

Printed and bound in the United States of America

Don't Quit

When things go wrong as they sometimes will;
When the road you're trudging seems all uphill;
When the funds are low, and the debts are high;
And you want to smile, but you have to sigh;
When care is pressing you down a bit—
Rest if you must, but don't you quit.
Success is failure turned inside out;
The silver tint of the clouds of doubt;
And you never can tell how close you are;
It may be near when it seems afar.
So, stick to the fight when you're hardest hit—
It's when things go wrong that you mustn't quit.

— Author Unknown

In loving memory of
Francis and Eloise McGlinchey

TABLE OF CONTENTS

PART THREE
MANAGING THE SELLING CYCLE:
Huddle Up! We've Got the Ball Now!

PART FOUR
SALES MANAGER'S HANDBOOK:
Six Principles of Sales Management

GLOSSARY

Acknowledgements

In the course of my twenty-five year business career, there are many, many people who I could acknowledge and whom I would like to thank for what they have taught me. For the past ten years as a business development consultant and professional sales trainer, my clients have not only been my students but they have also been my teachers. My training methods are only valid when my clients put them into practice and achieve growth. It is a wonderful feeling to know you have helped others reach a higher level of success and a greater feeling of self-worth and happiness.

I would especially like to acknowledge and thank my long-time assistant, Cynthia McMillan, who has been at my side through good times and tough times. Her support and friendship over the years have been invaluable to me. Her efforts in helping me pull this book together were monumental.

I would also like to thank my family for their love and support over the years: Barb, Drew, Jill and Molly. They have always been my motivation and have provided me with desire and "a passion for success."

Preface

Twenty-five years ago, after graduating from Purdue University, I began a career in professional sales. I was not immediately successful, nor have I always been successful, as a selling professional.

Time and experience in sales should produce knowledge. In turn, knowledge should produce improvement. Insights and systematic methods help retain knowledge and improve performance.

I'm honored to share my insights, experience and knowledge with you as it pertains to selling. Hopefully *Let's Put Some Lipstick on This Pig?* will reinforce some fundamentals of selling that you may already understand. With a bit of optimism, I think you will pick up some new insights and strategies, which can help you become more successful as you journey through your professional sales or sales management career.

A NOTE FROM THE AUTHOR
These Days

These days, I do not spend the majority of my time and effort in the corporate training world. Rather, my time and effort is now devoted to helping others realize their dream of self-employment or entrepreneurship as professional sales development consultants. The McGlinchey Group, along with its licensed and copy-written training materials, The McGlinchey Method, enables qualified professionals to develop a career path in teaching and training.

I have always enjoyed sales and, although I have been the president of a few different companies and have sat on numerous boards, I have always considered myself to be a salesperson. The past ten years have been especially meaningful to me because not only could I keep being a sales professional, I also had the wonderful experience of being able to teach and train thousands of salespeople in many different industries. It has been my experience that the formula for success in a professional sales career is similar from one industry to another. I have been extremely fortunate to have witnessed the growth and improvement of many of my clients. Even though my training and materials played a part in their growth, my clients were primarily responsible for their own growth. Thus, they deserve most of the credit.

I would love your feedback on this book. Also, feel free to contact me at www.McGlincheyGroup.com if you have an interest or desire to follow a career path similar to mine.

PART ONE

Managing Yourself:

You Are Your Most Important Client

CHAPTER 1

I See the Enemy Daily When I Look in the Mirror

*The definition of insanity is doing the same thing
over and over and expecting a different result.*
—Mark McGlinchey

We can all be better. We can all do better. Even the best salespeople in any industry have some room for improvement. Chances are, if you are reading these words, your profession is sales, and you are taking a step towards improving your game. Improvement is always created by change. In sales, improvement can happen in many different areas, although for the next several chapters, we're going to focus on self-improvement. What do you need to do? What changes do you need to make personally to become more successful as a sales professional?

Some of the topics we are going to discuss concerning self-improvement are not new or revolutionary. However, there probably will be some material you haven't thought about before. This information may open your eyes and take you to the next professional level.

In sales, you, the sales professional, are the biggest part of the process. In its simplest form, sales involves four parties—you, your company, the prospect and the prospect's company. Of these four elements, there is only one which you totally control, and that is you. So let's start to work on you.

☞ DENIAL

Denial is part of human nature. Most likely, there isn't a human being on Earth who hasn't practiced denial in some capacity of his or her everyday life. We witness denial on a daily basis. We see it in the people we love. We see it in the people we work with. Often in movies and TV shows, the plot or the subplot indicates denial. People in the media spotlight—athletes, entertainers, politicians—sometimes disgust us with their denial. Denial has caused wars, ruined governments and wrecked homes. In sales, "sales denial" has limited or ended careers.

If a person is not happy with his or her weight, oftentimes, that person will refuse to step on a scale to monitor his or her weight. He chooses to exercise denial. Until an alcoholic or drug addict seeks help for that problem, denial wins out in that scenario as well. Go to a Little League game, don't watch the game, just watch the parents. That is often denial extraordinaire.

Let's get back to the profession of selling and try to focus on how denial could be holding you back. Denial can manifest itself in many ways for the selling professional. The most dangerous or hampering form of denial is career "sales denial"—not recognizing the changes you need to make in order to be better. Denial hampers a person's desire.

Challenges are what makes life interesting; overcoming them is what makes life meaningful.
—Joshua J. Marine

Denial is the killer of success in sales; it is the negative. Desire is the stimulator of success; it is the positive. Let me give you my definition of desire as it pertains to sales. Desire is a passion for success. Desire is the engine which motivates you to make the kind of money you want to make, to win awards, to be recognized in your profession, to be sought after. Most importantly of all, desire to win tucks you in bed every night with a healthy feeling of self-worth.

I have trained thousands of salespeople in the last ten years. Naturally, when you have trained that many people, you've seen it all—the good, the bad and the ugly. I have yet to meet a very good or great salesperson that did not have an extremely high level of desire. It is the one common denominator I see in all great salespeople: their desire, their passion for success, which often translates into their money motivation. Attitude, commitment, work ethic, bravery, industry-knowledge, product-knowledge, a good rolodex and good selling skills are all important elements in a successful sales career. However, you can be weak or lacking in some of these areas and still be extremely successful, if you have a high level of desire.

Therefore, the first thing we need to work on is your desire: your passion for success. Desire is the fire. But denial is the fifty-five gallon drum of water which puts that fire out.

☞ A DENIAL STORY

In 1995, I was invited in to consult with and train a sales force for a high-tech network solution provider. Like a lot of Silicon Valley companies of their era, this company had gotten off to a very hot start a few years before when there was virtually no competition in the marketplace. Things move quickly in the Valley, and within two years, my client had to compete with four other companies in the market space, and sales were starting to flat-line.

Before I started the training, I interviewed the salespeople and the sales managers to get a handle on what problems were real and to customize my training so it would be as effective as possible. What I discovered was my new client (XYZ Company) had what I call "middle-of-the-pack" syndrome. This is when a company operates in a certain market space and is not the best, the latest or the greatest product out there. At the same time, they are not the cheapest or lowest end product or solution out there. They're caught in the middle—they're not the best nor the cheapest.

When a salesperson works for either the best or the cheapest within an industry, that person will experience success because, typically, buyers may buy either the best or cheapest. However, when your company has middle-of-the-pack syndrome, your sales force better be pretty damned good and be able to rely on good salesmanship more than the company's strong points to make sales.

In the case I'm referring to, the entire sales force and management team were deep in denial. When denial is at the helm, it will usually manifest itself in the form of excuse-making and finger-pointing. The sales team was blaming the company, its pricing structure and the competition. However, the real problem was "sales denial." This sales team did not possess what I consider to be good sales skills. They did not have a solid or systematic method of selling. Nor did they have good strategy or tactics. Yes, they were losing some sales due to middle-of-the-pack syndrome. However, more importantly, they were losing most deals as a result of their own lack of skills.

Through training and coaching, most of the sales team eventually realized what they had been denying: they could still win many deals in the marketplace even though they weren't the latest, the greatest or the cheapest by improving their skills, strategies and tactics. When denial is on its way out the door, desire to win is on its way in.

Exercise 1

In a blank notebook, begin to list all of the ways you exercise denial in your current job or career. How do you use excuses to cover up performance shortfalls? Focus on the denial that is affecting your performance in sales. Most importantly, focus on denial which could be affecting your desire or passion for success. After you have determined the areas where you have been in denial, then determine the effect it is having on your career and your performance.

Now, for you analytical thinkers, after you have determined these factors, put a pencil to what this has been costing you on an annual basis—a tangible, hard figure. Of course, no price can be put on how it affects your health, your happiness and your self-worth.

RESOLUTION

There is no miracle cure for "sales denial." The only way I know how to deal with it is just that—you have to deal with it on a daily basis. You have to force yourself to look in the mirror every day and ask yourself, "What am I denying today? What am I personally denying? What aspects of this deal that I'm working on am I in denial over?"

To eliminate denial, you must first understand that it's in all of us. It's human nature. You then must determine and come to grips with the areas where you are exercising denial. Understanding and recognition is most of the battle. You are now 90% of the way home. Dealing with it, correcting it and making the changes necessary to eliminate denial is the last 10%.

> *The soul is dyed the color of its thoughts. Think only on those things that are in line with your principles and can bear the full light of day. The content of your character is your choice. Day by day, what you choose, what you think, and what you do is who you become. Your integrity is your destiny . . . it is the light that guides your way.*
> —Heraclitus (c. 535-475 B.C.)
> Greek philosopher

BUILDING BLOCK # 1

Eliminate ➔ **Denial**

CHAPTER 2
Comfort Zone / Baggage

☞ *"TRANQUILITY BASE, THE EAGLE HAS LANDED"*

These famous words were spoken by Neil Armstrong as the Apollo spacecraft touched down on the moon. It was July of 1969, and the world watched in awe at the accomplishment of landing the first men on the moon. There is no greater example I can think of than that of Neil Armstrong being the right man, at the right place, at the right time. I once heard the definition of luck is when preparation meets opportunity.

To enjoy a professional sales career, you must first be in the "right place" and the "right time." Virtually no one can be successful, nor can he or she have the necessary desire and passion for success if that person is hampered or opportunities limited by forces or conditions which are out of one's control. It is also necessary for the situation to be real. It cannot be another exercise of denial.

If you do not believe in what you are selling, you should make a change. If you believe your products or services have little value, you should make a change. If you are capable of making more money than you are currently making, and your company's compensation plan is preventing you from doing that, you should make a change. If you have true philosophical differences with your company's management, you should make a change. If your integrity or moral values are compromised, you should make a change.

I'm not suggesting your time or place has to reach the level of perfection of Neil Armstrong's moon landing. However, it has to be adequate enough to fulfill you and keep you from constantly asking the question, "What if . . .?"

Working in an environment which does not afford you the growth and opportunity you truly desire will limit you. In fact, it will imprison you. For now, let's assume the time and conditions are right for you to get to the next level in professional sales. Only you can decide what the next level is. Is it career advancement? Is it higher compensation? Is it more personal freedom? Is it fewer worries? Is it a greater feeling of self-esteem?

> *The rung of a ladder was never meant to rest upon, but only to hold a man's foot long enough to enable him to put the other somewhat higher.*
> — Thomas Henry Huxley

☛ COMFORT ZONE

Comfort zone is the space in which we operate in our professional capacity. Yes, comfort zone applies to your personal life. However, we want to focus on your business or sales comfort zone. Often though, business and personal comfort zones do go hand-in-hand.

☛ A COMFORT ZONE STORY

Jim is a commercial real estate broker. His compensation is 100% commission. He has been a commercial broker for ten years. Like many other straight commission sales positions, his financial ceiling is unlimited and during his first three years in the business, the goal was simply survival. When Jim first got in the business, ten years ago, he and his wife, Nancy, did not have any children. Nancy earned $70,000 a year at her job—an amount on which the two of them could adequately live. The plan was for Jim, in his fourth year, to be able to produce $70,000 a year in income to replace Nancy's earnings at which time they would start a family. In year four, his income had reached $70,000. Now, he was the sole breadwinner in the family.

From years four through ten, Jim averaged $85,000 a year in income. A couple of those years were at $70,000 while he did have one year at $135,000. There are two other brokers in Jim's firm who outperform him, year in and year out. However, both have fewer years of experience and less knowledge than Jim. He had established the boundaries for his comfort zone—the professional financial space in which he was operating.

Jim's Comfort Zone

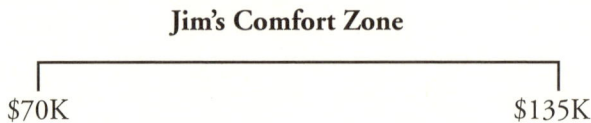

He was uncomfortable making less than $70,000 a year. Get ready and put your seatbelts on . . . he was also uncomfortable making more than $135,000 a year. Most of us have a comfort zone. Obviously, men like Henry Ford and Bill Gates did not. We will continue to operate in a space we are familiar or comfortable with. Jim realized that an annual income of under $70,000 was going to be very uncomfortable and create problems and concerns which he wanted to avoid. On the flip side, though, it's hard to imagine he would also be uncomfortable making more than $135,000 a year, but he was. There were a number of reasons for this discomfort:

1. Jim was from a working class family. Even though his parents were fine people, they tended to be suspicious of people they knew who had excess disposable income.

2. Many people in Jim's and Nancy's family were not doing as well as Jim was financially. The year Jim made $135,000, he and Nancy took a trip to Hawaii and also remodeled their house. To Jim's surprise, friends and family alike didn't congratulate him. Instead, he encountered negative reactions and envy.

3. Jim didn't want the burden of higher expectations placed on him which would dictate the new goal of $135,000 per year.

> *You are currently making exactly what you think you are worth. Not a penny less. Not a penny more. When you believe you are worth more, you will start making more.*
>
> — Napoleon Hill

Your present comfort zone may be too low to really achieve what you want in life and work. You may need to break out of your comfort zone and establish new boundaries. If you do this, you're going to experience some changes. You can't worry about these changes. You must embrace them. If your determined to escape your present comfort zone, here's what that will mean:

1. You'll come to realize you are a professional, and no different than a professional athlete, you must always be in training. Self-education and self-improvement in your profession are not a *sometime* thing, they are an *always* thing. You'll seek help from experts who can help elevate your game. You'll find you are reading fewer mystery novels and more books like this one.

2. You'll aspire to and try to emulate the very top people in your profession, and you'll keep telling yourself, "If they can do it, so can I."

3. You'll have goals (we'll get to that section later) and you will share those goals with your business associates, your boss, your spouse and even your children. Make yourself accountable to a higher standard.

4. The people you surround yourself with may have to change. You have to eliminate "drain" people—people who drain you of your positive energy or who will be envious or jealous of you rather than happy for you.

5. You will envision, dream and raise your goals. This will constantly force the bottom boundary of your comfort zone to increase.

Exercise 2

Determine the boundaries of your comfort zone. If you wish to move higher, establish a new comfort zone for yourself by moving the boundaries.

Now list all of the positive reasons or positive outcomes which will occur as a result of your new comfort zone.

Finally, list the implementation or changes necessary to reach your new comfort zone.

All things change, yet nothing is extinguished . . . there is nothing in the whole world which is permanent. Everything flows onwards, and all things are brought into being with a changing nature. The ages themselves glide by in constant movement . . . for still waters will never reach the sea.

— Ovid, 43 B.C.E. - A.D.E. 27

☞ BAGGAGE

Today, the term "baggage" is a popular cliché. When you hear the expression, "He or she has some baggage," it generally means that person is walking around with ideas or conceptions which are holding him or her back, causing unhappiness or preventing that person from further achievement. If you've been in the "sales wars" long enough, you are probably walking around with your fair share of baggage. Some of your sales baggage was given to you by your parents, teachers and other authority figures in your life as your young mind was being developed. The rest of your baggage can be credited to your prospects and some of your more difficult clients.

Bag # 1: Need for Approval

All human beings have a certain need for approval. Socially, this may be an admirable quality, but in sales, it can really hold you back. You don't need the prospect's approval. You need the prospect's trust and respect . . . there is a difference. From early childhood through our formative years, all of us have been programmed to seek approval. Our parents, our teachers and other authority figures had mechanisms in place for us to seek their approval. As we got older, we continued to seek approval from our co-workers, our loved ones and, of course, our bosses. In fact, I can't even think of a religion which isn't based on seeking a higher authority's approval.

Therefore, it is only natural in sales, consciously or subconsciously, for all of us to have a need for approval. We want to be liked and accepted by our prospects. The consequences of seeking approval from our prospects have a far-reaching effect on our sales efforts. In sales, when we're burdened with too much of a need for approval, we don't ask the tough questions we should be asking. We are constantly trying to avoid hearing the word "NO."

There are times when "NO" is the most important thing we can hear, particularly if our selling cycle lasts longer than it should, if our margins begin to shrink and if we have trouble closing. So we can forget about seeking approval when a sale is the main consideration.

Bag # 2: Discomfort Over Discussing Money

As a child, I can remember asking my parents questions which concerned money. Questions like, "Dad, how much do you make?" "Mom, what did our car cost?" "How much did our house cost?" and "Dad, do you make more money than Neighbor Jones?" These questions almost always brought a frown to my parents' faces and the message was coming through to me loud and clear—DO NOT talk about money, DO NOT ask questions about money. It's not polite. It's rude.

I'm in my mid-forties now and I am still uncomfortable discussing money. This too is probably an admirable social quality, but it's baggage you don't want as a sales professional. In sales, you have to openly, freely and without reservation talk about money. Far too many deals are lost because a sales professional did not openly discuss money with his or her prospects. It's hard to discover the hidden stalls and objections a prospect may have without discussing money. How do you uncover a prospect's budget or a competitor's quote or proposal without openly discussing money? It's pretty hard to sell anything, if we do not know whether the prospect has money (budget) and is willing to spend it.

Bag # 3: Disadvantages of Being a Super Consumer

The way we buy products and services as individuals will have a direct correlation or effect on how we allow our prospects to buy products and services from us. Let's assume you consider yourself a very knowledgeable and savvy consumer—you do a lot of research before you make a major purchase; you like to comparison shop for price; you clip coupons; you're more than willing to ask for a discount; you like to inform salespeople they are in fierce competition with someone else for your business. Congratulations, you're one shrewd consumer!

If you also happen to be a sales professional, it's time for a "consumer lobotomy." Everyone tends to see him or herself as normal. Thus, if you consider your own shopping habits to be "normal" consumer behavior, not only will you allow your prospects to do this to you, you will somewhat encourage it.

Bag # 4: Fear of Failure

This is closely related to Need for Approval. However, there is a difference. Need for Approval is baggage which gets in the way once the selling cycle is started, or once you are working a deal. But fear of failure is that awful baggage which prevents you from even leaving the starting blocks. The person who believes he will fail also believes the word "NO" will hit him like a .357 Magnum. Of course, it won't. You cannot win a race which you refuse to enter. I believe in the old adage "the sales professional who hears the most no's is also the sales professional who hears the word yes the most."

Ty Cobb set a record for the most stolen bases in baseball which stood for over fifty years. During the same season, he also set another record which still stands. This second record was for the most outs while trying to steal a base.

A great deal of talent is lost to the world for want of a little courage. Every day sends to their graves obscure men whose timidity prevented them from making a first effort.

— Sydney Smith

Bag # 5: Negotiating with Yourself

This particular piece of baggage is reversible, weather-resistant, can resist punctures, dents and scratches, and will fit in any compartment you like. Here's some of the conversation you may have with yourself which indicates you are carrying this bag:

"They surely won't pay our price."

"I must call on certain people in the organization and never call on others."

"I can't make calls on Friday afternoon."

"I can't schedule sales appointments for Monday morning."

"We're not competitive."

"I can't get to the decision-makers."

"I can't make a sale without making a top-notch presentation."

"They're going to need time to think it over in order to make a decision."

"They'll never share their budget with me."

"I can't get past the gatekeepers."

"They have no reason to be lying to me."

"No is permanent. It can never be reversed."

☞ CONCLUSION

Can you see how strikingly similar baggage on the part of you the salesman is to stalls and objections which you might hear from the prospects? However, baggage is not the stalls and objections you're hearing from prospects, but rather the obstacles you have in your own mind—even before you start working a deal. That's right. You're creating your own stalls and objections. The prospect isn't blocking you from making a sale. You're blocking yourselve from making the sale. You can't prevent a legitimate stall or objection which comes from your prospects. However, you can completely control your own sales baggage. Any time you begin negotiating with yourself, you need to ask yourself the following question: "Do I know this is an irrefutable fact?" Almost certainly, the answer will be no. Therefore, move the baggage out of the way and move forward.

> *If you know the enemy and know yourself, you need not fear the result of a hundred battles. If you know yourself but not the enemy, for every victory gained you will also suffer a defeat. If you know neither the enemy nor yourself, you will succumb in every battle.*
>
> — Sun Tzu (6–5th century B.C.)
> Chinese general.

BUILDING BLOCK # 2 & 3

Raise ➜ **Comfort Zone**

Get Ride Of ➜ **Baggage**

CHAPTER 3
Role Separation

There was that law of life, so cruel and so just,
that one must grow or else pay more for remaining
the same.

— Norman Mailer

Sometimes, our career (role) occupies so much of who we are that we aren't able to separate who we are and what we do as two entirely different issues. Everyone has a life outside of work, which has very little or nothing to do with his or her career. You probably have a family, a parent or parents whom you love and respect, brothers and sisters with whom you have a strong bond, a spouse and maybe children. You probably have interests outside of work. Chances are that you have hobbies and various activities where you like to spend your free time. This is you. This is the *real* you.

Your career or position as a professional salesperson is your role. If you can separate your role from you, the person, the process of selling becomes much easier. The concept of role separation is sometimes hard to put into practice. So let me share a story, which might help drive the point home.

JUNIOR PROM

In the Spring of my Junior year of high school, my friends and I were all looking forward to the Prom, and the parties and camaraderie which we knew would follow. A week before the Prom, my friend, Kenny, still did not have a date. I knew he really wanted to go but had been dragging his feet on the issue. He had already been rejected by a couple of girls who were going with other classmates. Another friend, Danny, was in exactly the same position as Kenny: no date and no prospects for finding one.

One day at the lunch table in the school cafeteria, Kenny, Danny, a few others and I were sitting around discussing the Prom. For some reason, the whole table was giving Kenny a hard time for not having the courage to ask some of the other girls to the Prom. Remember, Danny was in the same boat, however, the conversation at the table was focused on Kenny's lack of bravery.

Several tables away from us there was a group of female classmates. We knew their names but they didn't "hang" with our group, so we didn't know them very well. These girls were all attractive and fun-loving. So, I suggested to Kenny that he go over and ask one of them to the Prom.

Kenny said, "Which one?"

At this point, Danny spoke up and said, "No. Which one wouldn't you want to go to the Prom with?"

Kenny replied, "I'd go to the Prom with any one of them, but I'm not about to go over and ask them."

The next thing we knew, Danny jumped up from our table, walked over to the girls' table and proceeded to ask them, one by one, if they would be interested in going to the Prom with Kenny. The first one told Danny she already had a date. The second one told Danny she had a steady boyfriend who attended a different school. The third girl just gave Danny a flat no. Then, the fourth girl, Jennifer, said, "Sure. I'll go."

Danny grabbed Jennifer by the hand and marched her back over to our lunch table, as Kenny's face turned beet red. When he arrived back at our table, Danny announced to all of us that Jennifer would be going to the Prom with Kenny. As it turned out, they not only went to the Prom together, they also continued to date each other for the next couple of years.

On the other hand, Danny did not attend our Junior Prom. As a matter of fact, he never even asked anyone to go with him.

This situation was my first experience in understanding role separation. Danny completely separated who he was from his role, which was to find a date for Kenny. Since Danny was practicing role separation, he had no problem walking into a tough situation and asking tough questions. Most importantly, Danny was completely immune to the rejection which was dished out by the first three girls. When they told Danny no and rejected him, they weren't really rejecting him. They were rejecting Kenny.

In sales, if we can learn to practice role separation, our power increases ten-fold. When you use the telephone to try to set up an appointment, and someone rejects you, they are not rejecting you. They are rejecting your role. It wasn't personal, even if their tone of voice made it sound like it was personal. They were rejecting your company, your product or your service. During the selling cycle, if your prospect tells you no, again, they're not rejecting you as a person. They are rejecting your role as a sales professional. Far too many sales professionals experience paralysis because they cannot exercise role separation.

When you experience rejection in sales, let it fall on "My Role" and not on "Me."

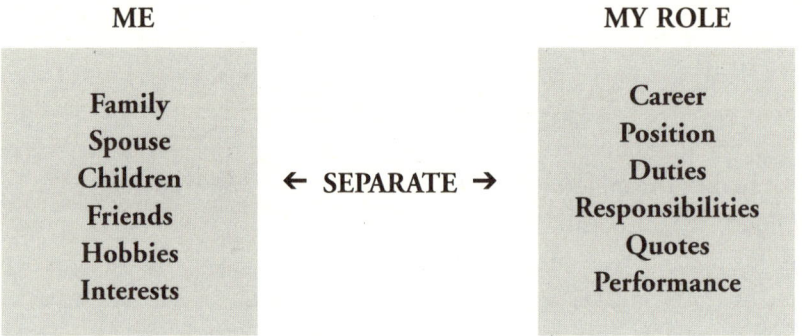

someone rejects you, they are not rejecting you. They are rejecting your role.

ME

Family
Spouse
Children
Friends
Hobbies
Interests

← SEPARATE →

MY ROLE

Career
Position
Duties
Responsibilities
Quotes
Performance

☞ EMOTIONAL SEPARATION

A large component of role separation is the ability to emotionally detach ourselves from any and all deals we are working on. When a sales professional is too emotionally involved in the selling process, more bad things can happen than good.

The ability to exercise role separation will dramatically affect your ability to exercise emotional separation. How many times in your career have you been working on a deal and you were so emotionally involved it seemed like a matter of life and death? You *had* to have this deal and you felt the consequences of not making this sale would be catastrophic. I'm sure you've been through this. I've been through it. Probably every salesperson has had this feeling at some point.

Sales professionals who have a tendency to become emotionally involved in the sale often worry, strategize on the fly, become excitable, exhibit mood swings and appear to be desperate in front of the prospect. Thus, the prospect realizes he or she controls the selling process. This shift in control will cause margins to shrink, and terms and conditions to be very one-sided. After a sales call, an emotionally involved salesperson might say to himself, "Oh, shoot! I should have said this, or I should have done that." This person wasn't able to execute during the call because he was caught off-guard as a result of emotional involvement. He paniced when a prospect asked a tough question or raised an objection that he wasn't expecting.

No single deal or sale will make or break your career.

Nor should it have far-reaching or lasting financial impact on you. If any one deal has a huge financial impact on you, then you are obviously suffering from a lack of sales activity. You are not putting enough deals in the pipeline.

> *Success is not a place at which one arrives but*
> *rather . . . the spirit with which one undertakes*
> *and continues the journey.*
> —Christian Science Monitor

☞ SEPARATING

Mastering role separation and emotional separation is very similar to dealing with denial, comfort zone and baggage. We're battling human nature and we're trying to reprogram ourselves to be professionals. That's tough stuff but if sales was an easy profession, everyone would be in it.

Practicing role separation boils down to understanding and attitude: understanding that who we are and what role is are separate components in life, and the the attitude of letting rejection fall on your role, not on you personally; any one sale or deal is not life or death.

Choosing the right words and phraseology can help you achieve and exercise role separation. Carefully select the manner in which you ask questions, respond to questions and make statements in sales relationships. Allow the customer the benefit of the doubt. Begin to phrase things in more of a tentative manner than a positive manner with your prospects. For example:

Wrong: "It appears our product is a good solution for you."
Right: *"I'm not sure our product is a good solution for you."*

Wrong: "My company and I could be of great benefit to you."
Right: *"You may not need us. It appears you have everything under control."*

Wrong: "Your current vendor can't do the things for you that we can."
Right: *"Your current vendor is pretty good. Why would you consider a change?"*

Wrong: "Our cost is more than competitive for the quality we provide."
Right: *"If cost alone is your only buying criteria, I'm not sure we're a good fit."*

Please note, I'm not suggesting you be negative. I'm suggesting you learn to phrase things in more of a tentative, even negative, manner than a positive manner. When you phrase things in an overly positive manner, two bad things can happen. First, your prospect can become combative since you're inviting them to disagree with you. Secondly, you're setting yourself up for emotional involvement in the sales process.

Role separation has nothing to do with your commitment or desire to be successful and win deals. It is simply a self-defense mechanism that keeps you emotionally detached from rejection or failure. This does not mean you don't want to make your quota, or blow-out your numbers. It means you have the proper perspective—you're okay if you didn't and you'll live to fight another day.

> *Your success story is a bigger story than whatever you're trying to say on stage . . . Success makes life easier. It doesn't make living easier.*
> — Bruce Springsteen

BUILDING BLOCK # 4

Practice ➜ **Role Separation**

CHAPTER 4
Destination

*Nothing happens by itself . . . it all will come your
way, once you understand that you have to make
it come your way, by your own exertions.*
— Ben Stein

Almost every salesperson has goals. Right? Almost every salesperson can clearly state their goals. Correct? Of course, almost every salesperson fully understands goals and how to set them. Yes?

Well, if you ask me, a lifelong salesperson who has spent the last ten years of his life as a professional sales trainer and consultant, I would disagree. Very few sales professionals have goals, the right goals, or understand goal-setting and its purpose. They even believe goals to be other things. Now, I would agree that most sales professionals have dreams—things they want to achieve personally, financially and professionally. Often, they confuse their dreams with goals.

Let's get on the same page in understanding what a goal really is. A goal is a dream with a plan. More specifically, a goal is a dream with a strategic plan. A goal necessitates exercising the proper behavior to carry out the plan. So let me ask you, do you currently have goals or just dreams?

☞ LIFETIME GOALS

I once remember seeing Coach Lou Holtz on a night time talk show discussing the fact that somewhere in his early adult years, he established something like 107 goals that he wanted to achieve. One was to someday be the head football coach at Notre Dame. He can now scratch that off the list. He also wanted to be the head coach of a National Championship team.

Again, scratch it off the list. He wanted to be on the Johnny Carson show, he wanted to write a book, he wanted to visit Europe, and on and on. At the point when I saw him being interviewed, I believe it was the mid-1990's, he had accomplished 88 of his 107 lifetime goals. WOW!!!

I believe it is impossible to establish professional goals or sales achievement goals without establishing lifetime goals first. Do you have a life plan?

> *Obstacles are those frightful things you see when*
> *you take your eyes off your goal.*
> — Henry Ford

☞ A LIFE PLAN

How can you possibly set any business goals for yourself, if they do not coincide with what you want to achieve personally? To set a goal for yourself to make $250,000 in any one given year, or every year, without having a plan for why you need that amount or how you are going to use the money is meaningless. Money or compensation which you would like to earn must funnel back to a plan.

☞ A LIFE PLAN STORY

One of my early clients, almost ten years ago, was a gentleman by the name of Jeff. He owned a company called Relocation Strategies, and had a small sales force which consisted of himself and three other professionals. When my training touched upon goals and life plans, I must have set off light bulbs in Jeff's head. I think he realized not having a life plan was the key element which was holding him back from further achievements in business and sales. Jeff's income was about $75,000 per year, which was at the low end of his comfort zone. He wanted to do better, he certainly had the ability to do better, the opportunity was there, but he had been stuck at $75,000 for three years. He was lacking the motivation to increase his income because he did not have a clear vision of why he wanted greater income. So, Jeff asked me to assist him in putting together a life plan.

When you put a life plan together, you need to revisit it every year in order to update it and possibly make some changes. As the years pass, you will find the things that are important to you can change. Therefore, the plan must also be altered.

The first thing Jeff had to figure out was when did he want to stop working and why. He was thirty-two years old and he determined he wanted to call it quits, work-wise, at age forty-five. His life plan reflected the reasons he wanted to retire from professional sales at age forty-five and his means of accomplishing that goal. We broke his life plan down into three different areas. The following is a brief description of Jeff's life plan:

A. Personal Accomplishments

- Triple the size of his company in the next thirteen years.
- Write a book.
- Provide private education for his children.
- Teach at a college.
- Run for Congress.

B. Lifestyle / Leisure Time

- Vacation with his family for one month each year.
- Own and live in a 5,000 square foot home.
- Own a lake cottage.
- Drive new cars every three years.

C. Financial Equation

Again, this is not Jeff's full-blown life plan, but rather an abbreviated version. Obviously, Jeff's life plan and achieving it was going to involve money. However, his life plan clearly stated how much money he would need to make on an annual basis.

It indicated that for the next thirteen years, to have the lifestyle he desired, he would have to start producing $120,000 per year in income. In addition, he would have to accumulate a warchest to provide for himself and his family after retirement. This increased the amount of money he would need to make each year for the next thirteen year from $120,000 to $220,000.

At this income level, he would be able to set aside $100,000 per year for his retirement which would continue to draw interest for the next thirteen years and beyond.

Finally, Jeff felt that after growing his business during those years, he would be able to sell it when he was ready to retire for an adequate sum. This money, combined with the income he had been putting aside for the past thirteen years, would enable him to retire and maintain the lifestyle he desired.

Life Plan Formula and Equation

List what you want to accomplish, the lifestyle you want to live, the leisure time you want to have and how you are going to spend it. Once these things are in order, you need to determine the amount of money necessary to fund your plan. Now, take into consideration the number of years you have left to work, or that you want to work. This will determine the annual income you need until you retire.

ANNUAL GOALS

Again, everything begins with a life plan. Annual goals and compensation goals have very little meaning, if they aren't part of a bigger plan. Your annual goals are really more of an annual review and adjustment to keep your life plan on track.

The purpose of individual goals is to keep you focused on a destination. Just imagine getting in your car and proceeding to drive for hours upon hours without a destination. You don't know where you're going or how to get there. The visual picture of someone just driving and driving all around town, up and down the highway, seems ludicrous. However, it's no different than a sales professional going through the daily motions of his job without goals. Goals also provide us with and remind us of the necessary actions required on a daily basis to find our destination.

Naturally, I've seen more than my share of salespeople who lacked courage or bravery; the ability to ask tough questions; the ability to plant their feet when necessary; and the ability to walk away from a deal rather than make a sloppy sale with low margins. Bravery in sales is doing what you have to do when you have to do it—even though you don't like doing it. What I've discovered, on a fairly regular basis, is that sales professionals who lack bravery do not have goals. The lack of a destination creates a lack of courage. There's no purpose in bravery if it does not have meaning in your life.

> *The difference between a successful person and others is not a lack of strength, not a lack of knowledge, but rather a lack of will.*
> — Vince Lombardi

Now is the time for you to exercise your bravery. It's time for you to begin developing your life plan. Once the plan has been developed, annual, quarterly, monthly and even daily goals will fall into place rather easily.

Exercise 3

Over the next few weeks complete a life plan for yourself. You cannot do it in one sitting. Begin by creating an outline of the different areas which need to be addressed in your plan.

For example:

1. Things you want to accomplish
2. Things you want to provide for your family
3. Your lifestyle
4. Your leisure time
5. Your financial security
6. Your retirement

All of these areas or categories should be broken down in fine detail. You must address a timeline—dates when you will arrive at your destination. You'll also need a road map, discussed in the next chapter.

▨ ▨ ▨

BUILDING BLOCK # 5

Chart Your ➔ **Destination**

CHAPTER 5
Road Map

*Setting a goal is not the main thing. It is deciding
how you will go about achieving it and staying
with that plan.*

— Tom Landry

A career in sales is a journey and, hopefully, the journey has meaning because you have a destination. Your life plan has determined where you want to go, what you want to achieve, why you want to achieve it and the quality of life you plan to experience. Your own personal road map will tell you how to get there. It's going to direct and monitor your behavior. This is the global positioning system which will keep you moving in the right direction on a daily basis.

Charting a road map is execution. It's taking well-conceived goals, or a plan, and putting them into action. A road map is worthless without a destination—and vice versa. Let's begin the journey and, hopefully, "we'll get our kicks on Route 66!"

☞ HABITS

A friend of mine, who has a Ph.D. in Psychology, once told me it takes twenty-one days to break a habit and twenty-one days to form a new habit. Is this a cold, hard fact or irrefutable theory? I really don't know. What I do know is that I respect her professional opinion and I believe this to be true: As long as you and I believe in the twenty-one-day theory, it will most likely work for us.

I have three simple daily habits which I use to try to stay on course to reach my destination.

Habit # 1: Just Do It!

Stop all procrastination—NOW!! If there is a duty or a task you planned to do tomorrow, yet you could do it today, do it. If there is something you were going to do an hour from now, yet you can accomplish it right now, do it. Procrastination is a virus which just keeps growing and growing. The more you procrastinate now, the more you will procrastinate in the future.

There's one thing every human being has in common, we were all given the same amount of time in a day. Bill Gates, the wealthiest man in the world, has twenty-four hours in his day. Unsuccessful people also have twenty-four hours in their day. No one has an advantage over anyone else in this area. We are all on equal footing. Therefore, success and accomplishment aren't based on time. They are based on how we use our time.

> *Even if you are on the right track, you'll get run over if you just sit there.*
>
> — Will Rogers

Habit # 2: Above the Line

There's a horizontal line (the trouble line) which stretches from eight o'clock in the morning until five o'clock in the evening, Monday through Friday—roughly the typical work day and work week. The trouble line represents the forty or so hours each week you have to be in front of your prospects on a sales call or on the phone trying to get an appointment with them. There are exceptions to the rule. You could be entertaining a prospect in the evening or playing golf with them on Saturday. For the most part, you have from 8:00 to 5:00, Monday through Friday, to be engaged in productive sales activities. There are only three ways to be above the trouble line—to be on the top side of the line, where everything happens, rather than under the line, where nothing happens.

1. Being in front of a prospect or an existing client trying to develop new business and, thus, new revenue.

2. Using the phone, trying to set an appointment, to get in front of someone to develop new business or new revenue.

3. Being on the phone with a third party (referral) which will lead you to get in front of someone to develop new business and new revenue.

That's it. These are the only three activities which put you above the line. Let's discuss all of the other activities during the course of a typical business day which you think may be valuable. However, these activities are below the line. The reason they are below the line is they are not directly leading to new sales, or they could be accomplished outside the 8:00 – 5:00 time frame.

Below-the-Line Activities:
- Writing proposals and preparing quotations.
- Sales meetings.
- Research.
- Product education.
- Developing sales and marketing materials.
- Strategizing with others.
- Lunch and coffee breaks.
- Driving (Unless using your cell phone to book appointments).
- Database mining.

Many of these below-the-line activities are necessary and have a purpose. However, these activities do not directly produce new sales or new revenue. Often when I work with salespeople and explain the trouble line to them, I will then ask, "How many hours each week are you above the line?" Most of the time, their off-the-cuff answer will be twenty hours or more per week. I will then drill down with a series of questions which helps both me and the salesperson determine that he or she is probably spending less than ten hours per week above the line. In many case, that salesperson is spending less than five hours per week above the line.

There is a huge correlation between sales productivity and time above the line. The more time you spend above the line, the more productive you will be and you will make more sales.

A few years ago, one of my clients determined he was spending roughly an hour a day above the line. He was in straight commission sales and his income, the previous year, was in the $60,000 range. He decided to do what was necessary to be above the line three hours per day, or fifteen hours per week. He did it!! His income the following year rose to $235,000. Being above the trouble line is *that* powerful.

Honestly assess yourself to determine how many hours each week you are above the line. After that, make the commitment to yourself to spend a greater amount of time than you currently are above the line. (Keep reading—some tools to help you are on the way.)

Habit # 3: Daily Journal

Start keeping a daily journal. There are only two times during the day you will use the journal—at the very beginning or your business day and at the close of your business day. Remember, if you can do this for the next twenty-one days, it will have become a habit and should stay with you.

Although the journal is simple, it is the most valuable tool I know to help you increase your time above the trouble line. The journal is also an excellent tool to keep you away from denial and it will force you to honestly assess your daily activities.

Daily Journal (example)

Action items for tomorrow: _____

_____

_____

_____

_____

Time spent above the line today?
_____ hours and _____ minutes.
Was I on compass today?___ Yes or ___ No.
What's the most valuable thing that I learned today? _____

_____

_____

When your business day ends, take five or ten minutes to work on your journal. The first section is action items for tomorrow. The items you list in this section can be both business and personal. What do you need to do tomorrow? What tasks do you want to accomplish? What actions do you need to undertake? This section is not a huge laundry list or daily planner listing every minute of how you will spend your day. Rather, it is a snapshot of two to eight things you need to get done tomorrow.

The next section is time you have spent above the line today. Recap today. How many hours and how many minutes were you above the line engaged in one of the three activities which directly lead to new sales?

Then, answer the question "Was I on compass today?" (Understanding compass is coming up.)

The last thing in the journal is to write down the most valuable thing you learned today. Most of the time, it will be about business but it doesn't have to be. Now, first thing tomorrow morning get your journal out and remind yourself of what you want to accomplish today.

A journey of a thousand miles begins with a single step.
— Lao-Tzu

☛ COMPASS

This is the tool or mechanism you are going to use on a daily basis to guide you to destination. Build the compass based on your goals and destination. For the next twenty-one days, work the compass. Then, hopefully, the compass will begin to work you.

☛ BUILDING THE COMPASS

Let's assume you have finished your life plan and you now realize your income must be $175,000 this year. Let's also hope and assume you are in commission sales. Thus, you have full control over your income and compensation.

Step 1:

Based on your life plan, how many days are you going to work this year? There are roughly 245 business days in the American work year. Let's assume that due to vacation and personal time, you plan to work 220 of those days.

Step 2:

What is the average commission you earn per sale? Let's pretend you sell software and each time you make a sale, the average commission is $3,500. If you have residual or renewal income, as you would in the insurance industry, you also need to determine what that income will be for the next 12 months. Without residual income, you would need to make fifty sales per year at $3,500 each.

Step 3:

You must determine your closing rate. How many prospects do you need to call on to make a sale? Let's assume your closing rate is 25%. Therefore, you need to call on 200 new prospects each year.

Step 4:

You need to understand your selling cycle. A.) From the time you open a deal, how long does it take to close it? B.) How many sales calls must you make on the prospect during that time period. For this example, assume your selling cycle is sixty days and it takes three face-to-face sales calls on one prospect to close the deal. Between Step 3 and Step 4, you will need to make approximately three face-to-face sales calls every two business days, or 1.4 per day.

Step 5:

How many contacts do you need to make in order to set one face-to-face appointment? Let's assume for every three people you speak with on the telephone, you are able to set one appointment. Therefore, you need to make 600 contacts each year, or 2.7 contacts per day.

Step 6:

How many times do you need to dial the phone in order to make one contact? Again, let's assume you need to dial three times in order to make one contact. The other two times you get voice mail or whatever. Therefore, you need to dial the phone 1,800 times per year, or 8.2 times per business day.

Assuming your numbers and percentages are correct, your compass now indicates: if you make 8.2 dials per business day, you should reach your goal of $175,000 this year.

It's that simple! It's that basic and it amazes me how few sales professionals have a compass. In this example, dialing the phone 8.2 times per day equals $175,000 in annual income. Again, if your calculations, projections and percentages are accurate—and they should be—then your outcome should also be correct. You should know yourself, your industry and your track record, and you should be able to come up with an accurate number to drive your activity.

Keep a close eye on your performance during the first ninety days or so of this new habit. Be prepared to adjust your numbers and your activity, if your initial assumptions and percentages were incorrect.

One more time . . . if you dial the phone 8.2 times per day, everything else will fall into place.

Now, let's combine your compass with above-the-line activity. Remember, in this example, you need to be on three face-to-face sales calls every two days. Let's assume a face-to-face call lasts for an hour and a half. Let's also assume it takes one hour per day to make 8.2 quality dials, which lead to approximately three in-depth conversations, which leads to one appointment. Therefore, every two days, you're spending over four hours face-to-face and two hours on the phone trying to get face-to-face. This equals over six hours. Now, divide this in half to determine your daily activity of over three hours during which you need to be above the trouble line.

Now that you have three new habits and your compass has been defined, you know exactly what your behavior needs to be—each and every day. You're not focused on any particular deal because you know things will work out. You're only focused on your compass and the necessary amount of time you need to spend above the trouble line.

> *The majority of men meet with failure because of their lack of persistence in creating new plans to take the place of those which fail.*
> — Napoleon Hill

BUILDING BLOCK # 6

Follow Your ➔ **Road Map**

CHAPTER 6
People Skills

Our mind is capable of passing beyond the divid-
ing line we have drawn for it. Beyond the pairs of
opposites of which the world consists, other, new
insights begin.

— Hermann Hesse

The topic of people skills is applicable not only in this section, where we want to improve your "inner game," but also later in the book when we will discuss strategies, tactics and skills. However, I want to get it out on the table right now because I strongly believe the first step to higher achievement as a sales professional begins with you and your inner game. These first six chapters are about self-improvement—issues we need to rethink, changes we need to make, traps we need to avoid and new skills we need to develop.

People sure are funny critters. Organizations like TTI, Ltd. and a few others have developed tests or profiles which indicate various differences in all of us. The TTI profile product called DISC breaks people down into four separate groups—Dominant, Influencer, Steady Relater and Critical Thinker. I've seen a number of variations of this test where the four categories are referred to as Driver, Social Being, Amiable and Analytical. If you were as familiar with testing and profiling as I am, you would be very comfortable with these findings. Each and every one of us will fall into one of these four categories.

Further explanation of these categories will fall in the *Happy Hunting/ Prospecting* chapter of this book. For right now, you don't need to understand them, you just need to understand that they do exist.

Each category represents not only a person's personality, but also that person's style, the way in which he or she goes about things, communicate and make decisions. Generally speaking, whatever category a person falls into, that person will most likely interact the best with other people who are in the same category. Therefore, for every four people you meet, you will naturally bond with one of them, and not naturally bond with the other three.

People skills have everything to do with bonding and rapport. Bonding and rapport occur when someone is comfortable with you and trusts you. It's not impossible but it is difficult to try to do business with someone with whom you have not established a bond and rapport.

☞ YOU ONLY HAVE ONE CHANCE TO MAKE A FIRST IMPRESSION

When you first meet someone, within the first thirty seconds to five minutes, the other person has made a subconscious appraisal of whether they trust you and are comfortable with you. This is true whether it's a face-to-face meeting or a phone conversation. Again, 25% of the time, you're in good shape. However, 75% of the time, just being you may work to your detriment. In that first thrity seconds to five minutes, if you have not established bonding and rapport (trust and comfort), you will encounter an uphill battle for the remainder of your selling cycle as you try to establish it—and you may never establish it.

The ultimate result of not establishing bonding and rapport is that your prospect will be defensive which will cause them to hide issues from you. They may not reveal their budget, they may mislead you and, yes, even lie to you.

Have you ever been to a social gathering, a business meeting or any other setting where when you first met someone, you did not like them or, more importantly, you did not trust them. Then, over time, you started to change your opinion about them. It is interesting that it took time for this to happen.

The problem in sales is often we don't have any time or enough time to enable someone to view us differently or change their original perception of us. Therefore, a good beginning is critical. Establishing bonding and rapport from the onset is vital.

People only see what they are prepared to see.
— Ralph Waldo Emerson

☞ DON'T BE WHO YOU ARE, BE WHO THEY WANT YOU TO BE

I'm certainly not advocating being a phony by misleading your prospects or completely trying to fool them. But I am advocating being an actor playing a role which enables your prospect to trust you and be comfortable with you.

The first way you do this is through mirroring and matching. There is no one in the world you are more comfortable with than yourself. There's no one's voice you've heard more than your own. There's no one's image you've seen more than your own. Everything you do and everything you think, you consider to be normal or typical.

Therefore, it only makes sense that we want our prospects to feel like they're looking in a mirror when they see us. The more they feel they are looking in a mirror, the more they feel you are just like they are, the more they will trust you and feel comfortable with you. To create this mirroring effect, you need to match what they do and how they do it.

☞ BODY LANGUAGE

Match your prospect's body language in every way possible down to the finest details. When that person shakes your hand, if they give you a power grip, give them one back. If their grip is light, make your grip light.

Walk the same pace they walk. Dress the same way they dress. I don't believe in the concept of "dress for success." I believe in the concept of "dress for your prospect." If I sold high tech computer equipment on Wall Street, most likely, I would always be decked out in a two- or three-piece suit. However, if I sold farm equipment, I wouldn't want to look like the Wall Street salesperson because I would look very much like a banker and farmers, for the most part, really don't care for bankers. My blue jeans, boots and Pendleton shirt may be the way to go.

You want to match your prospect's posture. If he's leaning back in his chair, you want to lean back in yours. You want to match his eye contact. You want to match his hand movements, if he likes to move his hands when he talks.

☞ TONALITY

Matching your prospect's speech is very important. Tonality is volume. Does this prospect speak softly or does she have a loud voice? Her tonality will determine your tonality. The softer she speaks, the softer you will speak. Of course, the louder she speaks, the louder you will speak.

I do not suggest trying to match speech accent. Often, this is derived from geography, culture or race. People in Texas do sound different than people in New York. People in West Virginia do sound different than people in California. Often Blacks, Caucasians, Hispanics and Asians do sound different from each other.

Trying to match an accent is very difficult and most likely will have the opposite effect of what you are trying to achieve.

☞ RATE OF SPEECH

Match the rate or speed of your prospect's speech. Just like tonality, this is an okay thing to do and I would advise it. If your prospect speaks very slowly, or slower than you do, you should reduce your rate of speech to match his. If this rate of speech is fairly quick, like a talk show host on television, you should try to increase your rate of speech.

☞ ENTERING THEIR WORLD

We have all been given five senses: taste, smell, touch, sight and hearing. We use our senses to survive, to learn and to teach and communicate. Human beings are the highest species on our planet. Therefore, we're the most versatile species in using our senses. We can even choose from time to time which sense we wish to apply to a situation. This isn't true of all species.

Let's take for example the white-tailed deer of North America. These beautiful animals flourish in abundance in our country since most of their natural predators are scarce. For the most part, only man remains as an unnatural predator to deer. Apparently, deer do not have great eyesight. Many zoologists believe they are color blind, in fact, it's been said a deer can only see for about forty yards with any clarity. After that distance shapes become more of a blur. However, a deer can hear the smallest sound up to a half a mile away and can pick up the scent of another animal, a human being or food sources from over a mile away. Therefore, it's easy to conclude that white-tailed deer primarily depend on hearing and their sense of smell as their primary survival and learning senses.

In the sales process, our prospects and clients also depend on their senses. In all liklihood, taste and smell are not the senses your prospects will be using to evaluate your product or service. Rather, they will be relying on their other three senses for their analysis. They will use these other senses— sight, hearing and touch—as learning and communication mechanisms.

Everyone, including your sales prospect, uses these three senses to take in knowledge and communicate. However, people primarily depend on one of the three more than the other two. If you can determine that primary sense, you stand a greater chance of entering a prospect's world.

Visual

People depend on their visual sense and, for the majority, visual is their primary learning sense. Primary simply means, if given the opportunity to learn or take in knowledge, most people prefer to do it visually. Of course, they use hearing and touch, but their sense of choice is visual. Certain industries and certain occupations make it very obvious what a person's primary sense is. Almost every engineer and architect is primarily a visual learner.

Audial

Audial primary learners are not as abundant as visual primary learners. An audial primary learner depends on hearing as his first choice mechanism for learning. The blind are obviously the ultimate example of a primary audial learner. However, others develop heightened audial learning awareness due to growing up in a noisy environment, having poor vision or even being dyslexic.

Touch

When someone is a primary touch learner, it usually indicates the information they take in will always be referenced back to a past experience. If you ever touched a hot stove as a kid, you'll never touch one again because you had a touch learning experience. If your prospect had either a good or bad experience with someone or some company you remind them of, they will associate that experience with you. A primary touch learner also relies on "gut feel" to learn and make decisions.

☞ UNCOVERING LEARNING SENSES

As I mentioned above, we all utilize seeing, hearing and touch to learn, communicate and make decisions. However, we all have a preference—a sense we prefer to use. Here is how you can determine your prospect's or another person's primary learning sense.

Let's assume I make a statement and someone wants to agree with and acknowledge my statement. They might respond in one of the following ways:

"I see what you mean," "I hear what you're saying" or "I feel the same way."

All three of these responses indicate agreement, but look at the words. The first statement is visual, the second is audial and the third is touch. Visual learners will often use visual words in their speech pattern—words and expressions, such as: "I see what you mean," "Picture this," "I envision this," "Can you draw it out for me?" or "Show me."

Audial learners will do the same with audial words and expressions, such as: "I hear you," "Sounds good," "That's a lot of noise," or "I'm listening."

With touch learners, the words from their mouth will be: "I have a good feeling," "I have a bad feeling," "It's been my experience" "I think," or "I believe."

A person's eye movement or eye contact can also indicate that person's primary learning sense. Visual learners have wandering eyes—like a kid in a candy store. An audial person will stare a hole right through you when you talk because he or she is listening intently to what you have to say. You'll notice touch learners like to use their hands—touch, feel, grab.

By using these discovery methods, you can usually determine a person's primary learning sense within five to ten minutes. Again, please note, primary is just that—their method of choice. They will and can use the other senses.

☞ HOW TO APPLY THIS KNOWLEDGE

Once you have determined someone is either audial, visual or touch, proceed to mirror and match. Speak a visual language, if they are visual. Use audial terminology, if they are audial. Of course, use touch terminology, if they are a primary touch learner. When it's time to make a presentation or get important points across, bring the information to them in their primary category.

Now, you realize true bonding and rapport does not happen by accident. It doesn't matter which one of the four categories you are in: Dominant, Influencer, Steady Relater or Critical Thinker, or what category your prospect is from, you will be able to establish trust and comfort because you have become them. You will speak his or her language, you will think that person's thoughts and you will have mastered both verbal and non-verbal communications. You have entered the prospect's world and he or she will accept you.

Exercise 4

Analyze five people in your life that you know very well, or with whom you have a lot of daily or weekly contact. Try to determine, based on your knowledge of them, what their primary learning sense is. Make a point in the next week or so to have at least a 5 – 10 minute face-to-face conversation with them to see if your analysis of them has changed. Of course, you will do this by paying very close attention to the words and expressions they seem to use in their pattern of speech.

BUILDING BLOCK # 7

Develop Your ➔ **People Skills**

SUMMARY OF PART ONE
Managing Yourself: You Are Your Most Important Client

I hope you picked up some valuable information in these first six chapters, or the section of the book I consider self-improvement. However, more important than gaining the knowledge is putting it into practice and making it work for you. The only part of sales process we completely control is ourselves. Every other part of the sales process is not totally within our control.

Again, in its simplest form, sales involve four parties—you, your company, your prospect and your prospect's company. If you can control or master 25% of that process (you), you're off to a pretty good start.

I'll finish this section with the same words I started with: *Insanity is doing the same thing over and over again and expecting a different result.*

Make the necessary changes to improve your inner game and use these seven building blocks as your foundation for greater achievements. Just as important is to begin building a greater satisfaction in your career. The greatest career I know of . . . a professional sales career.

> *Self-trust is the first secret of success, the belief that if you are here the authorities of the universe put you here, and for cause, or with some task strictly appointed you in your constitution, and so long as you work at that you are well and successful.*
> — Ralph Waldo Emerson

BUILDING BLOCKS

Develop Your ➔ **People Skills**

Follow Your ➔ **Road Map**

Chart Your ➔ **Destination**

Practice ➔ **Role Separation**

Get Ride of ➔ **Baggage**

Raise Your ➔ **Comfort Zone**

Eliminate ➔ **Denial**

PART TWO

THE BUYING CYCLE:

What's Going on in Their Huddle?

CHAPTER 7
The Scouting Report

You can't have an effect on something you don't understand.

— Dr. Michael Welsh

I have fond memories as I look back and reminisce about my days on the gridiron. I played on the defensive side of the ball as a strong safety. Every time a play ended, I can remember gazing at the other team as they were bunched up in a nice, tight huddle, knowing that inside that huddle a strategy was being formed, a plan was being determined and a play was being called. Their purpose in that huddle was to confuse us, mislead us and keep us off balance. Obviously, they knew what the next play was, but for me and my teammates on defense, we didn't. In football, I've always believed the offense has an advantage over the defense. This is due to the simple fact that they know what they're trying to achieve and what the play is, while most often the defense's only recourse is to react.

In major account selling, or corporate sales, the same thing often occurs. The professional salesperson is on defense wondering . . . *what's going on in the huddle?* The corporate "play book" (buying criteria) can be vast, flexible, cunning, misleading and mysterious. It can also be a moving target. I consider it to be virtually impossible for any sales professional to really know all of the plays in the corporate play book. However, I do believe it is possible to at least understand the players, their positions and the formations which they like to use.

This section is dedicated to helping you understand corporate buying criteria. I've read countless books, not just chapters, about corporate buying criteria. Most of the books I have encountered on this subject left me wondering, "Am I really in sales? This is more like engineering."

I think it is important to establish a few principles and theories about corporate buying criteria. After that, I also consider it important not to over think or over analyze the subject for two very good reasons: 1.) We will never know what play they are calling or if they're using an audible (changing the play in process); and 2.) It's out of our control anyway.

Let's begin to establish some useful knowledge concerning corporate buying criteria. The best place to start is with the players and their positions.

☞ CORPORATE FOOD CHAIN

All corporations and organizations, large and small, can be broken down into four groups of people or employees. These four groups (the food chain) operate without boundaries and beyond titles. Certainly, it's important in selling to understand the official organizational chart and to gather information about the people who are directly involved in a buying decision. Yet, a view of a chart does not tell you much about the power base of the organization. You must find the hierarchy or political/mystical structure of the organization. Unlike the official organizational chart, the food chain is usually unclear, barely visible and, often, is not discussed within the organization—despite the fact that it's existence is evident.

Frequently, sales professionals confuse influence (power) with authority (title). When in fact, the two are not necessarily synonymous. In the selling cycle, we often come across people who have influence (power) in the buying process but who do not have authority (title). These people may be secretaries, assistants or expediters who can either provide or deny you access which will allow you to penetrate their organization.

☞ HIGH TITLE / HIGH INFLUENCE

In a corporation, high title/high influence people are at the top of the food chain—the C-level, VPs, Directors, Department Heads, etc. Their title gives them authority and their influence throughout the organization gives them power. Often in the selling cycle, we don't meet or see these people. They may not be the person who tells us yes or makes the final buying decision but their veto power is undeniable.

THE FOOD CHAIN

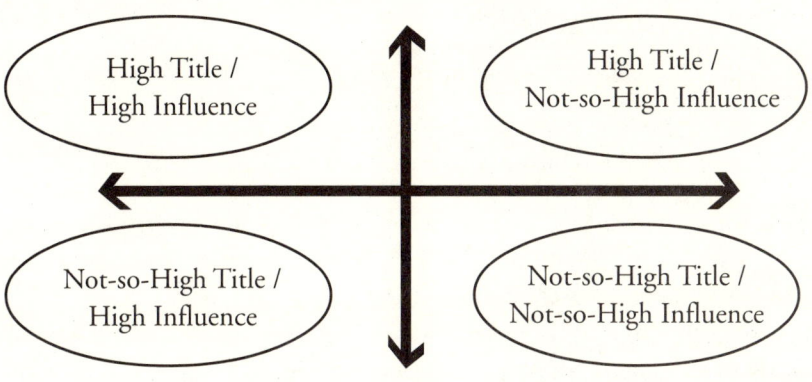

☞ HIGH TITLE / NOT-SO-HIGH INFLUENCE

Their title indicates they are fairly high up on the official corporate flow chart. Yet, they're really from the bottom-feeder level in the food chain, the unpublished political power structure in the organization. The best example I can give of someone in this category is the Vice President of Human Resources. There's probably a VP of Human Resources I haven't met or don't know about who shouldn't fall into this category. On the other hand, I personally haven't seen one yet who truly influences buying decisions.

☞ NOT-SO-HIGH TITLE / HIGH INFLUENCE

In the business world, the individuals driving the organization (High Title / High Influence) must create a support system for themselves. Delegation is a must. Through delegation, they extend their influence. Their loyal soldiers may not have a high rank (title). Nonetheless, these individuals possess high influence. They generally have earned their position in the food chain through past accomplishments. Often in sales, the majority of our time and effort is spent with people in this category. Frequently, the words out of their mouth will be "I really don't make the final decision" or "I'm not the decision-maker." This statement is not completely accurate, since their influence and approval is often critical for you to win a deal.

☞ THE NOT-SO'S / NOT-SO'S

These individuals have very little influence and very little power. Yet, they may still be of use to you in the selling cycle. More often than not, these individuals are easily accessible, willing to share their knowledge about their organization and can guide you toward the people you need to be in front of. In some cases, they may feel validated by having someone—even a salesperson or outsider—with whom they can share this information. You can also get inside the huddle with these people and gather information about things which may be going on behind the scenes—even information which is intentionally being kept from you. Be aware, your efforts with these individuals and their positive reception of your product or service should not be construed as true progress in the sales cycle. They are merely a source from which to gather information that will help to guide you forward.

☞ SUMMARIZING THE FOOD CHAIN

Identifying who the players are and what position they occupy in the food chain increases your chances of making a sale. Staying with the ol' football theme that has permeated this chapter, let me say it this way: We'll never see the play book but if we can understand the opponent's players, positions and formations, we're certainly more prepared to play the game.

> *The fastest way to succeed is to look as if you're playing by somebody else's rules, while quietly playing by your own.*
>
> — Michael Konda

☞ THE CHAMPION

In almost every organization, there's one person who is the champion. It's safe to assume the champion has high influence. At times, it can be very obvious who the champion is. At times, the organization (your prospect) itself is very aware of who the champion is. However, sometimes the champion flies below the radar screen and stays out of the public eye. He fights and wins his battles covertly behind closed doors—often without confrontation.

This person is able to work the organization from the inside out, while the sales professional is obviously trying to work it from the outside in. You will always find the champion where the action is. If the organization is making changes, the champion is probably involved. Strategic projects usually have the champion's fingerprints all over them. The champion usually operates more like a cat than a bull in a china shop. Be aware that the champion has usually earned the respect of people in the organization through past endeavors. Since they are so highly regarded, champions are well-networked throughout the organization. Thus, they're always "in the know" and are rarely surprised by events or changes.

When it comes to ethics, there is no middle ground for the champion—they are either very ethical or they are not. The champion is generally very much a political animal. In most cases, he or she will do what's best for the corporation, but in all cases, the champion will do what's best for himself. Unlike people in the organization who are bulls in a china shop (out to win battles), the champion is focused on winning wars.

Champions usually delegate very well, and the boundaries of authority do not get in their way when it comes to delegating. Champions are usually extroverts and have excellent communication skills. They know when to push and when to pull.

Many sales professionals have fallen off an unsuspecting cliff because they didn't find the champion or they were on the wrong side of the champion. *In corporate selling, it is an absolute must to identify the champion and to work with him or her more than with anyone else in the organization.* Naturally, you face a challenge if the champion and your buyer are not one and the same. If you, your product or your service has the support of the champion, you stand a pretty good chance of making a sale and winning the deal. If you don't have the champion's support, you are in trouble. If the champion is behind your competition, you're dead.

No one wants advice—only corroboration.
— John Steinbeck

☞ NEVER LOSE ALONE

I could probably name five or so strategic or valuable reasons why corporations form committees. In fact, the organization and the members of the committee can usually communicate to you very eloquently why the committee was formed and its value proposition. Frankly speaking, it's all a bunch of B.S. Most of the time, committees are formed for one reason, and one reason only—*no one wants to lose alone*. If a bad decision is made, if a project fails, or if the wrong path is taken, no single person wants the blame. Therefore, if it was a committee decision, everyone feels personally safe.

In truth, committees are a sales professional's nightmare, but often they are a harsh reality we have to deal with. When a committee is formed, which has anything to do with your selling cycle, the cycle will slow down. In sales, I've always believed in the statement, "time kills deals."

If an evaluation committee or purchasing committee is established, we have three choices. We can either ignore it, fight it or embrace it. At this point, embracing it is the best move possible. By embracing it, your prospect now sees you as a solution rather than as a vendor. You can try to turn a negative (a committee) into a positive by helping the committee establish criteria, timelines and methods of evaluation.

When working with a committee, you need to remove your sales professional hat and put on your "I'm a valuable consultant" hat. By assisting the committee, helping them establish criteria and even doing some of the due diligence and dirty work for them, you are in a position to establish criteria to your benefit and your competitors' detriment. You need to treat the committee as if it's a corporation of its own—by understanding the four categories of the food chain and applying them to the individuals in the committee. There's probably a champion on the committee but don't assume or take for granted that the committee's champion is also the corporate champion you must find. Often the champion sits outside the committee, but guides and influences the committee without being on it.

☞ A COMMITTEE STORY

Several years ago, I had a client that sold high tech networking and data communications hardware to large telecommunications companies. This client's average selling cycle was fifteen to eighteen months long. Once he found an interested prospect, it would be fifteen to eighteen months before the sale closed. His average sale was in the $2 – $5 million range and his commission was 5%. On one particular deal, not only did he embrace the formation of a committee, he even suggested it. He realized without the formation of a committee, he could not pull the people with the influence and power together in order to purchase his product.

He became a consultant, a special guest and a confidant to the committee. He was able to guide the committee in such a manner by helping them establish criteria and methods of evaluation. This did not speed up his selling cycle but absolutely made his product the only choice possible due to the criteria and evaluation methods. Even though the committee went through normal channels and evaluated his competition, it was simply window dressing. He did not win this deal because of his product. He won the deal as a result of his influence in establishing criteria. Therefore, his product was the only logical choice.

> *Capitalism needs to function like a game of tug-of-war. Two opposing sides need to continually struggle for dominance, but at no time can either side be permitted to walk away with the rope.*
>
> — Pete Holiday

CHAPTER 8
Stage 1—The Awakening

It's good to shut up sometimes.
— Markel Markeau

In May of 2000, I walked into a meeting (sales call) with Mark Jones and Steve Shubert of ABC Company, a publicly held corporation. These gentlemen definitely were part of the high influence area of the food chain. My products and services were sales training and consulting, and I was there to discuss how I could help their systems integration division. This area of the company represented over 50% of ABC's annual revenue and employed about fifty sales professionals.

Mark and Steve informed me that massive changes were on the way at ABC. One of the changes was a name change. The systems integration division would now be renamed to reflect their new direction. At the time, 85% of the revenue being produced by the systems integration group was in hardware or products, while only 15% of the revenue was attributed to consulting services. However, that 15% was producing over 80% of the annual profits within the division.

Steve and Mark informed me that under the direction of the CEO and the Board of Directors, ABC Company would have to slowly wean themselves away from unprofitable hardware sales while simultaneously growing their consulting services. They knew this process would take more than just a magic wand. They also knew this process of change would be an evolution. In addition, they realized, as did the CEO and Board of Directors, that the corporation might have to take two steps back before they moved three steps forward.

I was there because the ABC team realized that the sales force had to be completely reengineered and retrained. Their sales force was filled with people who knew how to sell commodities but who did not understand how to sell consulting services. I knew after the initial meeting that I had walked into an *awakening*—a situation in which a corporation realized they had a problem and they had to find a solution. Thus, they were in Stage 1 of the buying cycle—realization of a need. In this case, it was self-realization.

> *You can tell whether a man is clever by his answers. You can tell whether a man is wise by his questions.*
>
> — Naguib Mahfouz

☞ AWAKENING

When an awakening happens, an organization realizes there is a need for change. This need usually begins as dissatisfaction with existing methods, systems, services or vendors. During this stage, dissatisfaction grows until it reaches a boiling point. When dissatisfaction reaches a sufficient level of urgency, the buying cycle is underway. For most of my sales career, self-awakening has been the exception rather than the rule. Most of the time, I have had to create or inspire the awakening. However, when an awakening happens without your efforts and you simply walk into it, as I did at ABC Company, it's a wonderful thing. At least now I know why some people enjoy retail sales.

If your prospect is going through an awakening, the most successful step you can take is to ask a lot of questions and try to increase the level of urgency. When the prospect is in Stage 1, the worst thing you can do is offer solutions, make presentations or give them a proposal. They're not ready for it yet. You will appear to be pushy and, worse yet, you will appear to be stupid. Your prospect will be thinking, "How can you possibly be offering me a solution when you do not fully understand my problem?"

This is a time (the awakening) when most of the words coming out of your mouth should be in the form of questions. You want to be asking questions—not making statements or giving opinions.

The time to stop talking is when the other person nods his head affirmatively but says nothing.

— Anonymous

CORPORATE BUYING CYCLE: STAGE # 1

Awakening

CHAPTER 9
Stage 2—Due Diligence

*And while the law [of competition] may be some-
times hard for the individual, it is best for the
race, because it ensures the survival of the fittest in
every department.*

— Andrew Carnegie

Once the prospect's dissatisfaction has intensified to a point of urgency, and they fully understand that an existing problem must be solved, the prospect enters the second stage of the buying cycle. The due diligence stage is when the prospect's attention and actions are focused on uncovering and evaluating solutions. Often in major account selling, the due diligence stage will last longer than any other stage.

☞ *PRICE OF PRODUCTS AND SERVICES VS. COST OF OWNERSHIP*

The due diligence stage can be divided into three separate phases. This first phase is *Price of Products and Services vs. Cost of Ownership*. During this phase of due diligence, the prospect or buyer will reaffirm the awakening. More or less, they will second-guess themselves for the final time as to whether they need to proceed forward in order to solve a problem or prevent a problem from happening in the future—if that's what your product or service does.

Certainly, the prospect will weigh the financial considerations of moving forward vs. not moving forward. However, other factors besides money, budgets and profits will be calculated here. They will also take into account the effects that the problem is having on the employees, as well as, soft or intangible dollars or costs attributed to not solving the problem, such as turnover, job dissatisfaction, work load and discontent, which can grow like a fungus through a department or the entire company.

I can remember a selling situation in which there was no tangible justification for the purchase of certain hardware and software. The company could operate without it. The lack of these items was not adversely affecting the company's customer base or ability to operate in their market. However, the lack of this particular hardware/software package was having a devastating effect on a department of ten people who were forced to work a significant amount of overtime in order to accomplish their duties. The situation was creating tremendous job dissatisfaction and discontent which resulted in an extremely high turnover rate within the department.

The company's CFO determined the cost of turnover in this department was $82,000 per person. Calculated in his cost was downtime, transfer of work load to others, recruiting fees, HR advertising, management time wasted in the hiring cycle, training time, etc. The company could expect at least five people to turnover in the course of a year—thus, 5 X $82,000 – $410,000. The hardware/software solution was roughly $300,000. This is a good example of how the cost of ownership is less expensive than the price of products and services.

☞ COMMITTEES AND DELEGATION

As you see the prospect forming both formal and informal committees, and delegation about the issue starting to take place, this is a sure sign the prospect is in the due diligence stage. Since I have already discussed committees in a previous chapter, there's no reason to be redundant. My point is that committees are a way of life in corporate buying cycles. When we see them, we know exactly where we're at in the buying cycle—which is stage two, the due diligence stage.

☞ ENTER THE COMPETITION

Who opened the barn doors? Who released the flood gates? Why it was none other than your prospect! The prospect will now proceed to evaluate all of his or her available options. Unfortunately for you, your competition is an option. If you were around during the awakening, and your competition was not, at this point you have an advantage—especially if you helped create the awakening. Regrettably, the opposite is true as well.

> *Never lose a battle that's important, and never*
> *win a battle which is unimportant.*
> — Dr. Michael Welsh

☞ RUNNING THE GAUNTLET

Sales professionals can feel the most helpless during the due diligence stage. It seems the prospect is driving the car and the salespeople are just along for the ride. The deal or the sale is rarely won in this stage by doing the right things, but is often lost by doing the wrong things. Therefore, it's important to realize you are not pursing victory during the due diligence stage. But rather you are trying to maintain survival and stay in the ball game. The number of sales professionals who are fatally wounded during this stage is astronomical. They commit unwilling suicide through *premature presentation.* By doing this, the sales professional provides unpaid consulting and gives the prospect valuable information prematurely. This is information which will be used against the salesperson—information and knowledge the prospect can use as leverage with your competition to undermine your efforts. It's important in the due diligence stage for the prospect to realize you have all the cards—a full deck. However, even though the prospect believes you have all the cards, you haven't shown some of them to the prospect yet. You will, in time, but you need to hold some back to be used in the next stage.

Unwilling sales suicide also occurs when sales professionals do not realize the due diligence stage has started.

> *Knowledge speaks, but wisdom listens.*
> — Jimi Hendrix

☞ DEATH OF A SALESMAN

My trusted assistant, Cynthia McMillan, who serves as both an office manager and the CFO in my business, informed me several months ago that we needed to make some changes to our existing IT network. The awakening happened as a result of Cynthia's past experience and knowledge. She then proceeded to share the awakening with me. Thus, both of us were now awake. We invited three different vendors in to begin our buying process.

At the point which we invited them in, Cynthia and I were truly in the due diligence stage. The awakening stage was over. Two of the vendors/sales professionals spent their initial sales call with us (2 hours) discussing issues which seemed irrelevant. The ship had already left the dock and these two sales professionals did not realize it. The information they gave us, and conversations we had with them would have applied in Stage 1 and some of it would even have applied in Stage 3. However, Cynthia and I were firmly in Stage 2—the due diligence stage.

The third salesperson, consciously or unconsciously, realized where we were in the buying cycle. His products and services may not have been any better than the other two, but he understood us and exactly where we were.

"People buy things for their reasons—not yours."

The third salesperson exemplified this theory on his initial call. Obviously, the first two did not. I had the opportunity to witness firsthand, on the opposite side of the fence (as the buyer), the deaths of two salesmen. As noted before, the third salesman had survived. Victory was not at hand. He had not won the deal yet, but he achieved survival. Again, this is the main goal during the due diligence stage.

☞ WORKING THE STAGE

In conclusion, your first step as a sales professional is to recognize when your prospect has entered, or is in, Stage 2. In competitive situations, some of your opponents will fall by the wayside here—just because of their lack of understanding as to where the prospect is and not adjusting their sales strategies and tactics. The due diligence stage is the perfect opportunity for you to: 1.) Determine the food chain; 2.) Begin to work and develop the food chain; 3.) Identify the champion; 4.) Establish a working relationship with the champion; and 5.) Embrace the formation of committees you may be able to assist in establishing criteria which will ultimately make you the winner.

> *Sometimes the best presentation you'll ever make is*
> *the one you never had to make.*
> — Mark McGlinchey

CORPORATE BUYING CYCLE:
STAGE # 2

Due Diligence

CHAPTER 10
Stage 3—Appraisal

Once the prospect has obtained competitive alternatives, the buying cycle moves into the third stage—the appraisal. In this stage, last minute fears and concerns could arise which can block or delay a decision. Discussions with competitors can reopen. Sometimes, this stage is a non-event. For example: You might be a long-term supplier who has an excellent record within an account. Since the client or customer knows of your well-deserved reputation, the appraisal stage is merely a rubber stamp. Unfortunately, it is rare for this buying stage to be a non-event.

In complex sales, or deals with a long selling cycle, vendor perfection is rarely met. The survivors of Stage 2 (due diligence) now move on and differentiation begins to take place. The prospect entered this stage hoping for a perfect outcome, a clear-cut winner and a supplier with a flawless solution or more importantly, a supplier who eliminated any and all risk which could fall back into the buyer's lap.

☞ HOW PROSPECTS REACH A DECISION
Identifying Differences
The prospect will begin to differentiate the features and benefits of your solution along with those of the competition. This is often the prospect's view from 30,000 feet, rather than digging into fine detail on the ground floor. The most obvious differences between you and your competition are identified, such as price, quality, past performance and references, and meeting delivery dates or implementation points.

Importance of Differences
Once the element of competitive differentiation is out on the table, the prospect or buyer will apply an assessment criteria to the differences. He

or she will begin to drill down into the details of the differences and, more importantly, start to address the ramifications and results in worst case scenarios or situations. Then the prospect will assess: How realistic is the worst case? What is the chance of it really happening—great or small? If it does happen, how catastrophic is it?

Prioritizing Differences

Finally, after the prospect has a list of differences ranked in order of importance, the judgment process can begin. The prospect will compare the strengths and weaknesses of competing products and services. A pecking order of what's important is now in place. Let's pretend the decision criteria involves ten areas of differentiation. The prospect may break these areas down into two issues of great importance, four issues which would be helpful or nice to have, and four issues which are of little importance.

☞ THE CHAMPION IS IN HIS ELEMENT

Stage 3 (Appraisal) is the champion's stomping ground. He or she is helping to form and create decision criteria. This person is leading the way to insure their vendor of choice is going to come out smelling like a rose. It is very important for a selling professional to always have a pulse on the champion in this stage. If the salesperson is unable to take the champion's pulse, he must work the corporate food chain to determine where the champion stands. The information provided by the not-so's/not-so's during this stage is invaluable. Remember, these are the people who cannot influence decision but are extremely helpful to you in obtaining information.

☞ IF THEY SAY IT, THEY MEAN IT

When Stage 3 (Appraisal) is transpiring, the stalls and objections that the prospect relays to you are most likely real. Any good selling professional with years of experience in the "sales wars" realizes stalls and objections are commonplace. They happen in every selling cycle. They also happen in every stage of the buying cycle. Stalls and objections are the weapons and ammunition prospects use to keep us off guard, keep us in place and put us in a position to begin negotiating rather than selling.

The definition of selling is getting your price for your products and services. Negotiating is when you give up something for something else in return. Salespeople often give up something for nothing in return—that's neither selling nor negotiating. I call it bending over.

— Mark McGlinchey

There's a big difference between stalls and objections which are real and can prevent or kill a deal vs. stalls and objections which are not real and are merely negotiation tactics in disguise. Once again, if your prospect is truly in Stage 3, the stalls and objections most likely are real. Therefore, you must deal with them and try to solve them.

☞ LAND MINES

Known stalls and objections, real or unreal, are conventional warfare. Unknown or undiscovered stalls and objections which are real are land mines. You cannot affect what you do not understand. You cannot change what you do not know.

☞ A LAND MINE STORY

Aaron worked for a regional financial consulting firm which, years before, would have been considered a mid-sized CPA firm. Over the past ten years, the firm's business had evolved from tax preparation, audits and estate planning into other areas, such as asset management, wealth preservation and corporate profit management. Aaron's target market was small to mid-sized companies—in particular, the individuals at the C-level of these companies, or the owner of the company who was a successful entrepreneur. Often, CPAs, investment bankers, attorneys, etc. don't consider themselves selling professionals—as if they are above the fray and superior to the title. If they want to kid themselves, fine. But let's not kid ourselves. Somebody or some people in their professional organization must be developing new clients and producing new revenue.

In the course of his duties, Aaron unlocked a possible opportunity for his firm with the owner of a mid-sized manufacturing company. The organization had sales of about $100 million per year with 400 employees. His original opportunity was a result of the company's dissatisfaction with the current administrators and managers of their 401K pension plan. However, Aaron realized if he could get his foot in the door on this piece of their business, he would be able to parlay it into future business, encompassing many different areas where the company and the owner of the company could use his firm's services. This sale, this deal, this new account was Aaron's path to becoming a partner in the firm.

The buying cycle in this case had all the trademarks of being typical. There was an awakening and Aaron did an excellent job of intensifying the urgency. Through the due diligence stage, he was the frontrunner. Thus, he achieved survival. Now, in the Appraisal stage, he just needed to hang on and win. The problem was that his idea of hanging on in order to win involved ignoring signs of hidden or undiscovered stalls and objections. For the past few weeks, the prospect, who in this case happened to be the champion, had been a little less warm and receptive to Aaron. Aaron also noticed people in the corporate food chain with whom he was working, both with and without influence, were not returning his phone calls in a timely manner.

His biggest fear in this deal was the perceived greater expertise of larger national firms. The larger national firms had branding (name recognition) working for them. The senior partners in Aaron's firm had always told him, "Never bring up the competition. Never create your own stalls and objections. Ignore it and don't discuss it." The senior partners and Aaron believed, "Our firm is excellent at what we do. Just convey our message. We're not a bit scared of using references as referrals."

Aaron's biggest fear became reality. One of his competitors, a large national firm was able to overtake him at the very end of the Appraisal stage. The competitor had spent most of the buying cycle in second place behind Aaron, but succeeded in beating him by pounding on the only issue they thought could derail him. Aaron's firm had a solid reputation, fine credibility and expertise in pension administration but since Aaron and his firm chose to stick their heads in the sand, they hit a land mine. It was a stall or objection that was real and undiscussed. If he had chosen to deal with his biggest fear in this Appraisal stage, most likely he could have separated perception from reality. Since Aaron did not face his fear, the prospect's vision that perception was reality cost him this deal.

The moral of the story: Always address your biggest fear because it is usually like the elephant in the room which everyone sees but no one is talking about.

> *Courage is not the absence of fear, but rather the*
> *judgement that something else is more important*
> *than fear.*
>
> — Ambrose Redmoon

CORPORATE BUYING CYCLE: STAGE # 3

Appraisal

CHAPTER 11

Stage 4—Negotiation / Execution

A verbal contract isn't worth the paper it's written on.
— Samuel Goldwyn

It would be too simple to suggest that once the prospect has made a decision the buying cycle is over. In the corporate world, very few sales cycles stop when the contract is signed. Most sales involve implementation, possible installation, post-sales support and ongoing service after the sale which, if done correctly, will lead to future business. This fourth stage of the buying cycle is obviously what a sales professional would call the close.

Let us never negotiate out of fear, but let us never fear to negotiate.
— John Fitzgerald Kennedy

☞ NEGOTIATING

As a sales professional, when you have reached the fourth and final stage of the buying cycle, negotiations tend to intensify. While you are in Stage 3, stalls, objections and possible negotiations revolve around bigger issues. The negotiations in Stage 4 can center around small issues that the buyer will try to make you believe are large issues. The tendency for most sales professionals is to give in on all of these issues just to get the deal done. However, giving in on small issues can have a negative effect. When we concede or give in and get nothing in return for our concession, two bad things are happening: 1.) The prospect or buyer will tell themselves, "Maybe I should have asked for more;" and 2.) We have just trained the prospect or buyer to always ask for more in the future. Always remember, true negotiating is when you give something up for something else in return. Giving up something for nothing in return is not negotiating. Always get something in return. Even if it doesn't matter to you or your company.

☞ PRINCIPLES OF NEGOTIATION

1. *Handle your business issues without emotion.* When your personal feelings interfere with business, they cause frustration, cloud your judgement and can lead to failure.

2. *Avoid becoming a casualty.* Most sales professionals who negotiate poor outcomes set themselves up for future complications. When negotiating becomes part of the buying process or the selling cycle, there are no hard and fast rules. Every person has a different set of rules which can be subject to change. You become a casualty when you give up more than you or your company are comfortable with. This can create scars which we carry around as salespeople and can deflate our self-worth.

3. *It is what it is.* In the final stage of the buying cycle, you must deal with the reality of the situation, not what should have been or could have been; but rather, what it is now.

4. *Don't worry about what you can't control.* Always be aware of the stalls and objections that are real—the ones that can kill a deal. Your focus on perception vs. reality can get cloudy when you negotiate. Keep asking yourself, "What is perception? What is reality?"

5. *Never become a hostage.* Know when to walk away. Know where to draw a line in the sand. Be willing to call the prospect's bluff on stalls and objections that you know are not real.

☞ NEGOTIATING TACTICS

1. *The Flinch.* This is conveyed through body language or a look of disbelief on your face when asked for a concession.

2. *The Take Away.* This is when you imply that you want to revisit and

possibly take away concessions you have already made. The purpose of this tactic is to stop the prospect from continuing to ask for more.

3. *Offer Options.* Let's assume there are five issues on which negotiations are still taking place. Tell your prospect you can concede on two or maybe three of these issues but you have to hold firm on the others. Give them a choice on the two or three they want.

4. *Higher Authority.* Defer to higher authority. You cannot give them what they are asking for because it is not within your power and you will never get approval.

5. *Let's Pretend.* Use the verbiage, "Let's pretend, I conceded on this issue" and ask . . . *what happens next?* If what happens next is to your advantage, or helps finalize the deal, then you might think about conceding the point. However, if it does not move you closer, then why concede? And, tell your prospect that.

6. *The End of the World As We Know It.* This tactic involves taking your prospect to the edge of some terrible outcome and showing them you have the strength to walk away. Usually, both parties—not just the seller—have a great deal to lose if the negotiations fail in the fourth stage of the buying cycle.

7. *Truth Detector.* The use of flattery or humor in the negotiating process at the right time, or at critical times, can help you uncover how firm the prospect is on an issue and where the line can really be drawn.

8. *Standard Practice.* When your prospect is negotiating with you and asks for certain concessions, get used to using the terminology back to him or her, "This is not standard practice." This will begin to wear on the prospect. Very few people enjoy constantly breaking the law.

9. *Home Field Advantage.* In the final stage of the buying cycle, when negotiations are taking place, try to get the prospect to make a road trip to your office or facility. This tells you how committed they are to getting the deal done, which is to your advantage. It also, subconsciously, reinforces their commitment.

10. *Never Be Outnumbered.* Negotiate one-on-one or two-on-two. Try never to be caught in a situation where there are more of them than there are of you. If you ever find yourself outnumbered, always use the tactics "higher authority" and "this is not standard procedure."

BUYING CYCLE STAGES

STAGE	COMPELLING ISSUES DURING THIS STAGE	SIGNS THAT THIS STAGE IS OVER	COMMON STRATEGICE MISTAKES IN THIS STAGE
AWAKENING	There is a problem. How big is it? Action must be taken to solve the problem.	The prospect accepts and acknowledges the severity of the problem. Plans and actions are being put in motion to solve the problem.	Failure to investigate and fully understand the problem. Making presentations or offering solutions prematurely.
DUE DILIGENCE	What purchasing criteria should be established? What committees should be formed? Which vendors should be given the opportunity to compete?	Decision mechanisms are in place. Some of the competition has been eliminated.	Failure to uncover decision criteria. Failure to work the food chain. Failure to identify or influence the champion.
APPRAISAL	What are the risks of moving forward? Identify differences. Prioritize differences.	Large issues have been resolved. Real stalls and objections have been saitsfied.	Ignoring your biggest fears. Assuming victory. Not staying in close contact with the champion.
NEGOTIATION/ EXECUTION	Let's get everything that's not nailed down (greater concessions). Establish timeline. Set delivery dates.	Negotiations stop. Committees sit idle. Focus is now on delivery or implementation.	Becoming complacent. Not being as available. Making excessive concessions to get the deal done.

The object of war is not to die for your country,
but to make the other guy die for his.
— General George S. Patton

CORPORATE BUYING CYCLE:
STAGE # 4

Negotiation / Execution

SUMMARY OF PART TWO
The Buying Cycle: What's Going on in Their Huddle?

As I mentioned in Chapter 7, we could turn the buying cycle into rocket science, if we wanted to. In fact, we could break it down, dissect it, analyze it, slice it and dice it into small fragments. It could be a book unto itself, rather than just a section of this book. Countless books have been written about the buying cycle. However, it is my opinion that the section I have dedicated to it is all you need to know and what you need to understand. Anything beyond this would be overkill. I have often seen bigger problems created by over analyzing a topic than by not analyzing it at all. Furthermore, the buying cycle is generally outside the control of the sales professional. Yes, there are aspects which you can mildly control, and people and issues that you can influence. However, the process itself is controlled by the prospect. The next section will detail the things you do control as sales professionals.

CORPORATE BUYING CYCLE STAGES

The Awakening

Due Diligence

Appraisal

Negotiation / Execution

PART THREE

Managing the Selling Cycle:

Huddle Up! We've Got the Ball Now!

CHAPTER 12
Happy Hunting / Prospecting

Success consists of a series of little daily efforts.
— Mamie McCullough

If you've been in the sales world long enough, you should be familiar with the terminology of hunter vs. farmer. Well-seasoned and knowledgeable sales managers understand that salespeople can often be broken down into one of two categories—hunters and farmers—a salesman is either.

Farmers are sales professionals who are both skilled at and comfortable with working an existing customer base, servicing that customer base and developing new business from old or current customers. They are relationship managers. They work like ambassadors bridging their company with the client's company. The value a farmer provides for their employer is account management more often than generating new revenue. When a sales professional is referred to as a farmer, it is often an uncomplimentary statement. It means he or she lacks either the skills or the fortitude to perform the most difficult task there is in the sales world, which is prospecting. For many years, farmers have been commonplace in the sales world. However, little by little they are heading towards extinction. Most corporations realize the most important value a sales professional can have is the ability to find and develop new accounts.

A few years ago, I read a study conducted by the business school at a major university. The study indicated a typical U. S. business will lose 53% of its current customer base over a five year period. Think about that. It's frightening. For those of us in sales, it means most likely we will not be doing business with half of our customers five years from now. Please don't exercise denial by considering yourself to be non-typical.

Hunters on the other hand are sales professionals with both the skills and the fortitude to prospect for new business and new accounts. The majority of hunting jobs are straight commission without a ceiling on the sales professional's income. Generally, hunters have a greater sense of urgency than farmers. They are typically more results-driven. They are almost always held in higher esteem by their employers than a farmer would be. Hunting jobs can usually be found in abundance since demand is much greater than supply. Hunters are not necessarily smarter, more knowledgeable nor more skillful than farmers. However, the one advantage hunters have over farmers is their ability and willingness to prospect. That's HUGE!

> *Through my many years of sales management and sales training, I have seen salespeople with great skills and great knowledge fail because they could not prospect. Conversely, I have seen salespeople with average talents who could and would prospect become very successful.*
>
> — Mark McGlinchey

☞ SECRETS TO SUCCESSFUL PROSPECTING

Secret # 1: Recognition and Understanding

You cannot be successful at prospecting and cold calling, if you do not recognize and understand the reasons why it is so tough. As I mentioned in

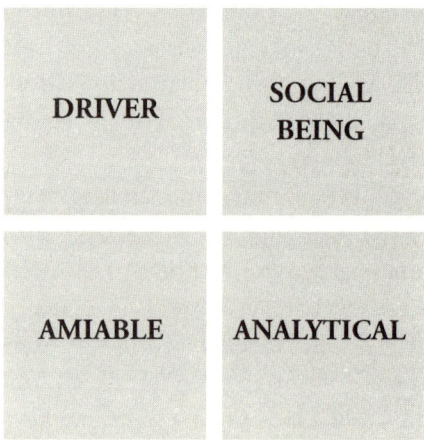

Chapter 6 (People Skills), everyone can be placed into one of four categories according to personality and personal makeup.

Drivers

These are results-oriented people. Usually, they have a dominant personality but always with a dominant makeup. They see the world in black and white. They like to be in charge and like to be the leader. They can be volatile. However, they rarely hold a grudge or allow problems to fester for a long period of time. Typically, drivers are also able to make quick decisions. These people could be extroverts or introverts.

Social Being

These are "people people." They enjoy the companionship and camaraderie of other people. Social beings tend to be name-droppers who enjoy the trappings of popularity. They would rather be at a social gathering than spend quiet time alone. Nearly always, social beings are extroverts.

The Amiable

These individuals do not like conflict or confrontation. They are comfortable with a daily routine and are very habitual. Generally, these people do not welcome change and frequently do not adapt well to changes which do occur. These are easygoing people. It takes a lot to light their fuse. Once it happens, they do not get over it quickly. They can hold a grudge and have a very long memory. These people can be extroverts or introverts.

The Analytical

These are very detail-oriented people. Like the drivers, they are also interested in results. However, they are just as concerned about the process to achieve the results. They are slow to make decisions and operate very carefully. Analytical people are usually much more concerned about risk than reward. Generally, these individuals are introverts but not always.

Who am I?

The following is a quick and fairly accurate test or evaluation to determine which of the four categories you fall into. (My training organization uses a much more elaborate test to help people figure out who they are. However, I am confident this quick test will most likely provide an accurate snapshot.)

Read the eight statements listed below. Then decide which statement most accurately describes you and which statement least describes you.

A. Tense, focused, competitive, out to win

B. I know what I want and I go after it

C. Likeable, fun, people are drawn to me

D. Strong relationships in my life are important to me

E. Calm, steady and operate with consistency

F. The peacemaker, I get along with almost everyone

G. Strategic, systematic, its important to understand the process

H. Results are important, but the means and the ways to get results are just as important

---

Who Are You?

If you are most like A or B, you are a driver.

If you are most like C or D, you are a social being.

If you are most like E or F, you are amiable.

If you are most like G or H, you are analytical.

On the other hand, your responses to the second part of this exercise will show you who you will have the most difficulty dealing with in a professional (sales) or in a social situation.

Drivers are the most natural hunters. They have the ability and mentality to prospect. However, only 12-15% of the population is made up of drivers. Due to their makeup, drivers don't carry around as much baggage which keeps sales professionals from prospecting.

Social beings are burdened with the "need-for-approval" baggage. When it comes to prospecting, their need for approval will get in the way because salespeople receive very little approval when prospecting.

Amiables can be paralyzed by the "fear-of-failure" baggage. They would rather not begin a process which could result in failure.

Analyticals carry around the "negotiating-with-yourself" baggage. Over-analyzing and procrastination get in their way of prospecting effectively.

Life Scripting

We are products of our environment. Consciously or usubconsciously, we have been tremendously influenced by the authority figures in our lives. Mainly, we're influence by the authority figures from early in our lives—parents, teachers and older siblings. Much of their influence resulted in a script—a pattern of behavior or thought processes which will play out for the rest of our lives. For example: I was the youngest of seven children from a working-class family. It was important in our household that food was never wasted. At mealtime over the years, I heard my mom tell me thousands of times, "clean your plate." That is now scripted with me. I always clean my plate—even if I'm not that hungry or if I don't particularly care for what I'm eating. The script endures. Each of us probably have scripts playing in our heads which make prospecting even tougher, such as: "never talk to strangers," "children should be seen and not heard," "only speak when you are spoken to." Often, the scripts we have are helpful in a social environment but can be paralyzing when it comes to prospecting.

A Scripting Story

A few years ago, I had a meeting with Jim Leonard, who was the managing partner of one of the nation's largest residential real estate firms. Naturally, I was there to discuss training. During the course of the meeting, Jim became fairly emotional when he talked about why so many people fail in residential real estate. He could not understand it since he had been such a successful residential realtor himself. As you know, success in residential realty has everything to do with successful prospecting.

Jim said, "Mark, I don't understand this. We bring people into our business. We provide the best training possible. We layout a complete roadmap for them to follow, which tells them how many phone calls they need to make every day, how many business cards they need to pass out each week, lists of various organizations to join and network in. All they have to do is follow the roadmap and most of them don't; 80% of the people who come into our business fail."

I sat back for a second before I responded to Jim. Out of his office window, about 100 yards away, was a mini-mart—a combination small supermarket and gas station. I said to Jim, "If I handed you a weapon right now, would you go over to the mini-mart and rob it? Threaten the cashier with the weapon?"

He responded, "What kind of question is that?"

My reply was, "It may seem like a stupid question, but what's your answer?" Of course his answer was no. My next question was . . . *why not?*

Jim proceeded to tell me robbing a convenience store would be far outside his moral and ethical boundaries. It was illegal and he would not break the law. This activity completely represented who he was not. It was not part of his makeup to do anything like that.

I told Jim that in sales there are people who think that prospecting and cold calling feels like robbing a convenience store. Prospecting is an activity which is way outside their comfort zone. Scripts subconsciously go off in their heads which paralyze them from prospecting. It didn't matter how good their training or roadmap was, if your salespeople could not recognize and understand what was emotionally happening to them when they tried to prospect, they would not be able to deal with it and make the necessary corrections.

Secret # 2: Role Separation (refer to Chapter 3, if necessary)

Who we are and what we do for a living are two separate components in our life. We must be extremely conscious of this fact when we prospect. Prospecting is generally 90% failure and 10% success. To accept the failure, we must constantly tell ourselves, "The prospect is not rejecting me. They are rejecting my role or my company, but not me. And, I'm okay with that." Be emotionally detached from your prospect. Have a mindset that you are in the third person. You're not asking for yourself, you're asking for a third party—your role or your company.

Keep one eye on your compass (Chapter 5)—the most basic thing you have to do on a daily basis to reach your destination or goals. If you keep an eye on your compass, it's easy to develop emotional detachment.

When prospecting, always think back to a job or an activity which you absolutely hated. Compare that much hated job to the prospecting activities necessary in your current career. With this as a point of reference, it's easy to tell yourself prospecting isn't so bad.

During college, I had a job one summer where I was a hod carrier on a construction site. The job was dirty, messy, hot and I spent most of the day with 100 pounds of wet cement draped on a tray across my shoulders. Any time I go to prospect now, and I'm trying to manufacture an excuse as to why I don't want to do it or don't need to do it, I always say to myself, "It beats carrying hod." This gives me the strength to move forward and begin prospecting.

Secret # 3: A Good Thirty-Second Commercial

All sales professionals should have what I call a good thirty-second commercial. This is to be used mainly via the telephone in order to set an appointment with an unknown prospect. You don't want to sound like a stereotypical salesperson in your commercial—telemarketers or salespeople calling you from brokerage houses. You need to sound different and not like a salesperson. The thirty-second commercial must be canned. You could give the commercial in your sleep and you can do the commercial even when you're not at the top of your game. Since it is canned and very repetitious from one call to the next, it will provide you with great role separation and emotional detachment. Although it is canned, *your thirty-second commercial cannot sound canned.* The commercial must be tactical. The definition of a tactic is a skillful maneuver to achieve one's objective. We will discuss various sales tactics in Chapter 19 and do an exercise to develop your thirty-second commercial at that time.

Secret # 4: The Clock Is Ticking

You can never recover time that you have lost. If you don't prospect today, you never know what future dollars you have passed up. Today is the day, and right now is the moment for you to set the appointment that leads to the biggest sale or deal you have ever done.

Pick the same time and same place every day for prospecting. Good hunters realize prospecting is a habit. You are either in the habit of doing it daily or you're not. Sales professionals who try to do their weekly prospecting all in one day rarely succeed.

"Friday. Yes, all day Friday, I'm going to prospect all day and set all of the appointments I need for next week." This doesn't work. If we're going to prospect consistently, we have to do it daily. The best way to do it daily is to plan to do it at the same time every day. Let's assume your compass calls for you to spend two hours a day on the phone prospecting which is two hours above the trouble line. Arrange your schedule and set your appointments around prospecting—not vice versa. Maybe you're going to prospect from 7:30 – 8:30 every morning, then from 4:30 – 5:30 every evening. Or, you might plan to prospect every morning from 7:30 – 9:30. The same place is also important—the same desk, the same chair, etc. This helps you turn prospecting into a habit.

During the time you spend prospecting daily, your energy should be high and your emotions need to be low. Good prospecting burns up a lot of energy—especially when you're tactical and not just winging it. To make daily prospecting a successful habit, you need focus. You cannot be easily distracted, which means you're not accepting incoming phone calls during this time; you're not constantly refreshing your coffee unless your pot is sitting right there; you're not engaged in any office conversation with others. When you're prospecting, nothing else is happening in your world.

Secret # 5: Goal Setting

When you prospect and cold call, your goals must be activity-driven and time-driven—not results-driven. The law of averages will work out over infinity but it will not necessarily work out on a daily basis. In one day, dialing the phone ten times could result in ten future appointments or sales calls. In one week, dialing the phone fifty times could result in zero appointments or sales calls. You must trust the compass you built in Chapter 5 and trust the law of averages/infinity.

When prospecting, the wrong thing to do is set a goal for the number of appointments you want to set. The right thing is to have a goal of how long you will spend prospecting each day or how many dials you will make.

Secret # 6: Contact Management System

You need to use or develop a contact management system, which will enable you to be a successful hunter. Being disorganized leads to procrastination. Over time, the mushrooming effect is that you will stop prospecting. Often, prospecting is timing or luck. You contacted a prospect at the exact time they were going through an awakening. Thus, you got an appointment and, hopefully, made a sale.

Maybe you contacted a prospect who was not at this stage. At this point, they had no need for your products or services. However, they just may have a need for them in three months, six months, a year or two years from now. You must put the company in a database so you can call back from time to time. Depending on your industry or situation, it could mean you will call them back monthly or twice a year. Without a contact management system (such as Act!), you are losing potential future sales and commissions.

If you're an Analytical, you are really good at using this type of system. However, don't be so good that this becomes an excuse which slows down your prospecting, because you want it to be so perfect.

If you're a Social Being, there's a strong likelihood that self-organization or using a contact management system will be a personal weakness, which means you need to place great importance on this activity.

The 6 Secrets of Successful Prospecting and Cold Calling

1. Recognition and Understanding
2. Role Separation
3. A Good Thirty-Second Commercial
4. The Clock Is Ticking
5. Goal Setting
6. Contact Management System

I am not discouraged because every wrong attempt discarded is another step forward.
— Thomas Alva Edison

CHAPTER 13
A Selling Strategy

As the proverb says, "a good beginning is half the business" and "to have begun well" is praised by all.
— Plato

A strategy is a plan or method of attack. It is our hope and intention of how we execute. For my first fifteen years in sales, I did not have a consistent selling strategy. Every sales call was a little bit different. At times, I may have felt like I had a strategy, but, for the most part, I did what I believe the vast majority of sales professionals do, which is wing it.

When a sales professional just wings it, he shows up on a sales call or works a selling cycle without a methodology, which will affect outcome. Terms like "Whatever happens, happens," "I can handle it," "Let the chips fall where they may," "Because I can think on my feet" are used a lot by salespeople who do not have a sound strategy.

Unlike my first fifteen years in the sales world, I now realize the importance of having and executing a selling strategy. I consider it vital to have an organized, planned process in which a salesperson proceeds through his selling cycle with his prospect or account.

To win by strategy is no less the role of a general than to win by arms.
— Julius Caesar

☞ BENEFITS OF A SELLING STRATEGY

Repetition

The more you repeat a process, the more proficient you become at that process. It's difficult to master anything without repetition. Do you want the doctor whose surgical procedure is a little different every time to operate on you? Or, would you prefer the doctor who has honed his skills and process through repetition.

Control

It's extremely difficult to control anything, including a sales process, if you don't know where you're going or how you're going to get there. Sales professionals who do not have a selling strategy usually relinquish control to the prospect. Thus, the prospect who is in control of their buying cycle is also now in control of the selling process. You become a passenger who is along for the ride.

Shorten the Selling Cycle

Without a strategy or a process, you are wandering aimlessly through the selling cycle. However, with a strategy or plan of attack, since you know where you are going and what you hope to achieve, the journey is usually much shorter.

Clear Understanding

A strategy allows a salesperson to have a clear vision of where he or she stands each step of the way. It also clears up the mutual mystification, which can happen between sales professionals and prospects as to . . . what happens next? You can't manage what you can't measure. A strategy is a measurement tool.

Accident Report

A strategy provides self-accountability and a mechanism for you to file an accident report. When you don't make a sale, you can analyze what, when and how you went wrong. You can retrace your steps and learn from your mistakes.

The next chapter will help you learn and understand a selling strategy, which will work for you regardless of your industry or the length of your sales cycle.

CHAPTER 14
Problem Zone

*Excellence, then, is a state concerned with choice,
lying in a mean, relative to us, this being determined by reason and in the way in which the
man of practical wisdom would determine it.*

— Aristotle

Try to visualize your selling cycle as a series of rooms or zones, which you must enter and pass through during a sale. From the time you first meet with your prospect until the sales cycle ends, you must navigate your way through each of these rooms or zones. Each room represents a different stage in the sales process, requires different navigational skills and will require varying lengths of time to traverse.

The first zone is the Problem Zone. This is by far the biggest zone of your selling cycle, and your selling strategy always begins here. There is a great deal of work to be done in this zone and typically you will spend 50% of your time during the sales process in this area to insure it is handled correctly. It is also necessary to remember, if you do not give this zone the necessary attention, and if you do not obtain all of the information or the right information required, you might never move forward at all.

From the prospect's point of view, the vendor who best understands and can solve their problem is the one who should get the sale. The more time you spend in this zone, the more likely it is you will close the deal.

What We're Trying to Achieve in the Problem Zone

Your basic goal in the Problem Zone is to *discover* and *intensify* the most compelling reasons why you have an opportunity to do business with this prospect. *More importantly*, you must help your prospect discover those compelling reasons on their own. You cannot and should not attempt to tell the prospect what their problems or compelling reasons are. You should help guide them to this discovery by asking questions. People and corporations do not buy products and services. They buy solutions. It's difficult to sell a solution if your prospect does not have a compelling problem, or if they don't understand the problem.

Let's pretend for a moment that for the past few weeks you have been feeling ill. So, you decide to consult with your family physician. You arrive at the doctor's office. The doctor walks into the examination room and greets you, and more or less asks you why you're there and what's bothering you. You reply, "Doc, I just haven't been feeling good."

Imagine your doctor responding to you in one of the following three ways:

1. He says, "Okay. I'm going to write this prescription for XXX. Go to the pharmacy, get it filled and get back to me in a week or two if you're still not feeling good."

2. He replies, "Okay. Let me tell you a little bit about me and my medical practice" The he proceeds to ramble on about his credentials, education and training.

3. He begins to ask a series of questions. "Tell me more. Is it a shooting pain or an ache? Are there certain times you notice it? Do certain activities bring this pain on? Has this ever happened in the past? Have you done anything to solve the problem previous to this appointment with me?"

If the doctor's response was # 1, you would probably be in disbelief and might even consider calling your state's medical board to have his license revoked.

If his response was # 2, you'd probably think he was a jerk and you'd still be confused as to whether he understood your problem or not.

Obviously, # 3 is the correct way for him to handle the situation. By asking the right questions, so he can make an accurate diagnosis.

The doctor-patient example is very similar to how you and your prospect make your way through the Problem Zone. The only difference is that the *doctor* is trying to diagnose the problem. In the sales cycle, you are working with your prospect to diagnose the problem *together*.

> *Disaster comes from the mouth.*
> — Chinese Proverb

Common Mistakes

Obviously, you should concentrate on developing a technique, it is equally important to avoid mistakes and looking like an amateur. Too often, salespeople can make all the wrong moves in the Problem Zone, such as:

1. Doing too much talking and not enough listening. Salespeople should be doing 20% of the talking and 80% of the listening.

2. Making statements and voicing opinions. If you're doing 80% of the listening, then the 20% of the talking you're doing should be in the form of questions.

3. Asking the wrong people the wrong questions. Discovering the company's mission is important; however, if you ask the head of purchasing what the company's mission is, he will most likely tell you to spend as little money as possible in order to improve profitability. Once this is stated, he can immediately use price as an objection.

4. Not doing your homework. There is a tremendous amount of basic information which can be gathered from outside sources about most companies. Since you have a limited window to interface with your prospect, don't waste it by gathering information you can get elsewhere.

5. Becoming consumed with wanting to make a presentation. You cannot and should not make a presentation if you don't fully understand the prospect's needs.

6. Being overly concerned with establishing credibility. Until a prospect has done business with you or anyone else, credibility is merely hearsay. By asking the right questions, gathering the right information and operating in a concise, organized manner, you will establish more credibility than you would ever be able to with product literature or premature presentations.

7. Acting over-zealous in conveying your company's value proposition. Again, you should not bombard the prospect with irrelevant information. Your company's one and only value proposition which the prospect will care about is *solving their problem*—PERIOD.

8. Being determined to communicate features and benefits. If the features and benefits don't solve the prospect's problem, they are irrelevant. Don't waste time talking about irrelevant information. *People buy for their reasons, not yours.*

☞ HOW TO WORK THE ZONE

You may want to reread the Chapter on Awakening to help reinforce the ideas which might prompt a prospect to take action to solve a problem. The Problem Zone is all about cause and effect, and discovery. As I stated before, if you're working this zone correctly, you will do 80% of the listening and 20% of the talking, primarily in the form of asking questions. Even if you already know the answer, you should ask that question. The prospect must hear the question, reach their own conclusion and voice the answer aloud. Once the issue is out of the prospect's mouth, it most likely is a "real" problem. You must continue to drill down with additional questions in order to discover if the issue is the most compelling reason you have to do business with the prospect's company.

It is important to be aware that when a sales professional asks a lot of questions, prospects can become defensive. It's important to note: your questions must be nurturing and non-aggressive. Your prospect cannot feel like they are downtown at the police station being grilled. Therefore, you should be asking open-ended "why" and "what" questions, such as: "Why is this a problem?" and "What has been the effect?"

☞ PLAN YOUR QUESTIONS AND OBJECTIVES

Before meeting with a prospect, take an objective look at your products and solutions. Also, look at your existing client base. What problems do your product solve? How can you save the prospect time, money, effort or reduce stress?

Think about the questions you need to ask to have the prospect find these same issues in their own operation. For example, let's assume your product, in the corporate world, generally solves one of three main problems. Let's pretend the first problem it solves is reducing down time. Plan to ask the prospect questions concerning down time—how much, how often, how expensive it has been, what other departments is it affecting, what effect is it having on other people in the corporate food chain, what effect will it have in the future, etc. Then ask these same types of questions about the two other issues which your product usually solves. Plan your approach, define your objectives for each call, devise your list of questions and, if necessary, practice them aloud.

When working the Problem Zone during your selling cycle, it is possible to ask your prospect hundreds of questions. No salesperson can make a premeditated list of hundreds of questions to ask. That's impossible.

Therefore, it is important to make a list of what I call master questions. When you ask a master question, it may create a situation where you will ask a series of many, many questions, before you get to the next master question.

For example: Let's assume your first master question is "Tell me more." The prospect's response could dictate that you may ask many more questions before you ever get to master question # 2, "What is the cost associated with this problem?"

Exercise 5

Use the following list of sample questions to develop your own set of basic questions to ask a prospect in the Problem Zone.

1. Tell me more.

2. What is the cost associated with this problem?

3. If the situation continues, what effect is this going to have on your business? Six months from now? One year from now? Two years from now?

4. Is it a priority to solve this problem? How high is the priority? What is the timeline?

5. What are you currently doing, or what have you done in the past, to solve this problem?

6. How do you feel about this situation?

7. If I had a solution, would you want to work with me to solve the problem?

☞ EMOTIONAL VS. INTELLECTUAL QUESTIONS

Your questions can be broken down into two categories: emotional and intellectual. Although a certain amount of intellectual fact-finding is necessary, you should also concentrate your questions on emotional issues. If you find an "emotional hot button" from your prospect, stay with the issue. Emotions generally indicate compelling reasons to take action.

For example: If the head of a department is constantly on call due to antiquated equipment, you should not only ask questions about the problems the company is experiencing, you should also ask questions about how it is affecting his or her life. You may discover their nights, weekends and family life has been disrupted.

Often the most compelling reason action will be taken is due to personal pain rather than corporate pain. The company's compelling reasons will always be discussed in committee meetings. However, often the personal compelling reasons, which are not discussed, are what really drives the sale. From an intellectual perspective, the prospect knows that some form of action is necessary. However, it is their emotional response which will drive the process.

Please remember, you are an actor playing a role. If you appear to be emotional or show emotion to mirror and match your prospect, that's acceptable. This validates their reaction, helps to build additional bonding and rapport, and reinforces to the prospect that not only do you *understand* but you also *feel* his or her pain. However, you're in control of the process. You may be showing emotion but you're not personally feeling it.

☞ CORPORATE PROBLEMS VS. PERSONAL PROBLEMS

Most problems boil down to corporate issues and personal issues. On the surface, corporate issues will be openly discussed. For instance: We need to save the company money; we need to increase capacity; etc. However, personal issues and problems will have a far greater influence on the sales process. If you can give the prospect a solution which will prevent midnight phone calls from their production line, they will become emotionally invested in buying and implementing your solution.

COST AND CONSEQUENCES

Ask questions to discover the cost and consequences of the problem. Find out what will happen if the problem remains unsolved. This could include:

- Hard dollars
- Intangible dollars
- Lost customers
- Lost employees
- Unhappy customers
- Unhappy employees

All of these issues could lead to an emotional, compelling reason, which will cause the prospect to take action. Remain alert and read the prospect's expressions and body language. If you find a reaction, drill down on it with additional questions. Determine if this is a big enough reason to take action, or perhaps just one of several reasons which will prompt action.

A PROBLEM ZONE STORY

About seven years ago, I was training a client which provided datcommunications hardware. My client would have been considered a "luxury automobile," while their next closest competitor was basically an "economy car." During training, my client was working on a deal that had a $5 million price tag. The competitor was proposing a $2.5 million solution.

We began to work on a strategy to turn the issues into an "emotional, personal problem" for the prospect which was our only chance to win the deal. During the sales process, the rep discovered his prospect, the Director of IT (the champion), was dealing with bandwidth issues, system crashes and excessive downtime (all corporate issues). By digging deeper, the salesperson discovered that the champion was receiving midnight phone calls, working long hours, working weekends, missing Little League games and enduring marital difficulties as a result of the problems. These were emotional, personal issues.

The salesperson did an excellent job of discovering and intensifying emotion with the champion, creating trust, which enable the champion to believe that my client was the best possible solution. In truth, the competition's product would have solved the problem as well. Our salesperson worked with the champion, gave him enough information and ammunition to work the deal behind the scenes, justifying our high price tag. Of course, behind the scenes, the champion was conveying corporate reasons for our solution, but it was his own personal compelling reasons which were really driving the sale.

> *A good listener tries to understand thoroughly*
> *what the other person is saying. In the end he may*
> *disagree sharply, but before he disagrees, he wants*
> *to know exactly what it is he is disagreeing with.*
> — Kenneth A. Wells

MATCHING THE PROSPECT'S BUYING SYSTEM WITH YOUR SELLING STRATEGY

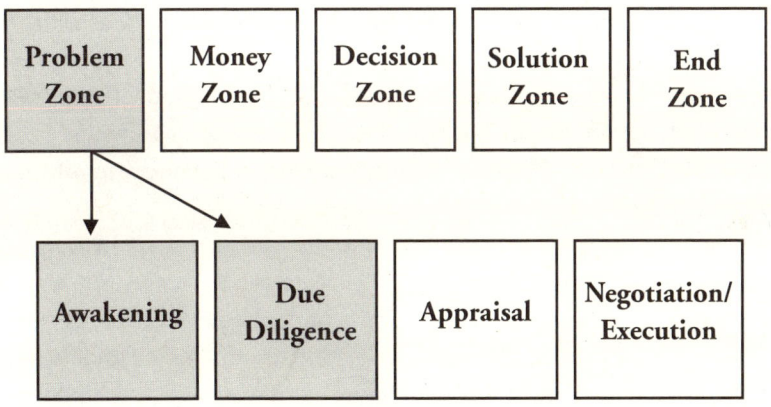

When the prospect is in the Awakening stage, and in the beginning stages of Due Diligence, your selling strategy dictates that you should be in the Problem Zone. You should be discovering and intensifying both the intellectual and emotional compelling reasons which can help you make a sale.

CHAPTER 15
Money Zone

Not everything that can be counted counts, and
not everything that counts can be counted.
— Albert Einstein

When working the Money Zone, the most obvious things that a sales professional is trying to discover are "Does that prospect have it?" and "Will they spend it?" Even though uncovering the prospect's budget is obviously part of the Money Zone, there's more work than that to do here. A sales professional needs to uncover all economic issues, not just the prospect's budget.

☞ A PROBLEM IS COSTLY, A SOLUTION IS AN INVESTMENT

Much like the Problem Zone, the best things that can roll out of your mouth here are questions—especially situational questions. Your goal is to help your prospect discover the cost of the problems; don't say what you think the costs of the problem are. All problems, which cause an Awakening for the prospect, have both a hard and soft cost. Naturally, the hard cost represents obvious, tangible dollars. On the surface, the soft cost would be conditions and situations. However, beneath the surface, financial ramifications can be uncovered.

Most selling professionals never uncover the soft costs. Often, the soft costs can be more compelling than the hard costs and can provide a greater leverage when the prospect is analyzing cost of the problem vs. cost of the solution. Get used to thinking and using the terminology with your prospects "investment." Your products and services are not a cost. They are an investment. Solutions are an investment. The prospect is not buying your products or services; but rather, they are investing in your solution.

I'm not interested in a return on my money, but
rather a return of my money.
— Will Rogers

☞ THEORY OF MONEY

The statement I am about to make will leave your sales manager breathless: *Stop trying to get your prospect's money. You are not out to sell anybody anything. You are on a sales call to try to uncover a problem for which you, most likely, have a solution.*

Theory # 1

Much of what you need to discover and know about money and budget will naturally occur in the Problem Zone. Financial information will usually come pouring out, if you are working the Problem Zone correctly. The less concerned you seem to be about discovering money, the more likely it is your prospect will unguardedly give you this information. If your questions about money and budget are too direct, or are untimely, you will appear to be needy or pushy. The prospect could become defensive and build an invisible wall of resistance. This will prevent you from understanding the necessary financial issues and information.

Theory # 2

I dislike the term "value proposition." Too many books and sales training sessions refer to value proposition. I'm sure you've read or you've been told, "It's important for you to convey your value proposition." No. The most important thing for you to do is to help the prospect understand that your solution is much more economical than living with the problem.

Theory # 3

If all economic (money) issues are out on the table early in the selling cycle, they are less likely to become a stall or an objection at closing time. Towards the close of a selling cycle, most prospects will use money like a hammer. They will beat on the salesperson for economic concessions realizing that late in the sales cycle a salesperson and their company are so fully invested in the deal, they'd have trouble walking away. As a sales professional, if I'm going to end up in a street fight with my prospect over money, I would rather do it early in the process before I have too much time and energy invested. By dealing with money early in the selling cycle, you defuse this issue as a stall or an objection which can arise at closing time.

☞ A MONEY STORY

In 1995, I was proceeding through my selling cycle. My prospect was a well-known and widely recognized brokerage house/investment firm. I was trying to do a deal where I would train a number of their Midwest offices, or sales professionals. Through the problem and money zones, I discovered these offices made up a region. The Midwest region was producing $60 million a year in commissions. The company had a two-thirds/one-third split with their salespeople/brokers. Thus, if a salesperson generated a dollar in commission, they earned thirty-three cents of that dollar, while sixty-six cents went to the house.

Eventually when I reached the End Zone (the final stage of my selling strategy), money became an issue. Remember, $60 million in commissions were being produced by this region with $40 million going to the brokerage house. My proposal called for a $200,000 investment in my training and the prospect was having trouble swallowing my $200,000 pill. They started focusing on issues which were really non-issues, such as: what was I charging per hour for my work, how much profit was I making and how much was it costing per head for the training. We finally reached the point in the discussions where I needed to make a point. However, even when you want to make a point, the best way to do it is in question form. So I asked, "Is this really a money issue? Or a conviction issue?"

Their response was, "What do you mean?"

Now I could make my statement. "If my training helps you produce 1% growth, that equals $400,000. If my training helps grow your business, that's an additional $4 million in commission to your firm. If the results of my training only produces 1/2 of 1% in growth, that's $200,000. Thus, I have to produce 1/2 of 1% of growth to pay for myself, and anything over 1/2 of 1% is profit that you will reap. It appears to me that we don't have a money issue. We have a conviction or belief issue. You obviously don't believe the training will yield 1/2 of 1% in growth. If you did, the cost would actually be an investment and you would be eager to spend the money. Therefore, let's get off of the issue of me reducing my price and let's get to the real issue—your conviction or belief that the training will be successful."

This statement and the explanation "Money isn't the issue, conviction is the issue . . ." stopped them dead in their tracks. In the end, I had to take them back to the problem zone to bolster their conviction. They became comfortable that the training would produce 1/2 of 1% in new growth and really had the expectation it would produce 10% new growth. Therefore, money was no longer an issue.

The moral of the story is understanding any and all financial and economic issues, and being able to leverage the issue at the right time where the investment in the solution is dwarfed by the larger cost of having the problem remain unresolved.

> *People have to be secure to transfer their money to you. Never forget that. How you make them secure is to not come at them from above telling them how marvelous the product is and how marvelous you are. Instead, work on their comfort zone first . . . leading things along effortlessly by asking questions.*
>
> — Stuart Wilde

MATCHING THE PROSPECT'S BUYING SYSTEM WITH YOUR SELLING STRATEGY

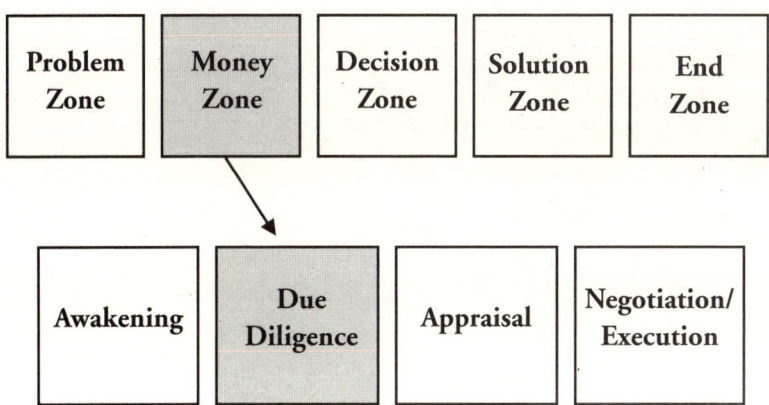

When the prospect is in the Due Diligence stage, your selling strategy dictates that you should be in the Money Zone, uncovering not only the prospect's budget but all economic issues which will have an effect on your ability to make the sale.

Chapter 16
Decision Zone

*He who asks a question is a fool for five minutes;
he who does not ask a question remains a fool for-
ever.*

— Chinese Proverb

In professional sales, the supplier who helps the prospect understand how to make choices is likely to have more of an impact than the supplier who is trying to sell features and benefits. Simply put, I believe in most competitive sales situations, the salesperson who best understands the prospect's decision process will usually win the deal.

When working the Decision Zone, our objective is to understand everything we can possibly understand about the prospect's decision criteria and decision process. We can apply Who, What, When, Why and How to our investigative process concerning decision. We should also be aware of the various elements that can affect a prospect's decision criteria.

DECISION CRITERIA

The Prospect May Set Criteria Prematurely

Many organizations establish decision criteria even before they have identified compelling problems. This criteria will constitute some of the minimum standards, which a supplier will be required to meet before being placed on a vendor list. Then, if a need arises, the organization will review the vendor list and decide who should be invited in to compete. This screening process is sometimes political. Vendor screening is not the only example of premature decision criteria. Often, corporations establish criteria before the full scope of a problem has been defined.

Prospects Have Pre-existing Decision Criteria

Even though this is closely related to premature decision criteria, there are some subtle differences. The evaluation methods and processes, which the prospect used in the past to buy similar products and services, will probably be repeated during current and future decision cycles.

Need Influences Decision Criteria

If the prospect is trying to solve a compelling problem, which is in unfamiliar territory for them (new problem), the decision criteria may continue to evolve throughout the decision process. Only when the prospect fully understands the problem and all available solutions are they likely to establish fixed criteria.

> *Adapt yourself to changing circumstances.*
> — Chinese Proverb

Decision Criteria Lives on Long After the Sale

As with pre-existing criteria, the decision methods—processes and expectations that your prospect develops—will most likely influence future purchases of similar products.

☞ HOW TO WORK THE DECISION ZONE

Again, your objective in this zone is to understand Who, What, When, Why and How:

1. Who will make the decision and who will have the greatest influence?
2. What factors will drive the decision?
3. When will the decision be reached?
4. Why is the decision necessary?
5. How are they going to reach the decision?

Over the years, I have managed countless salespeople who had a lot of time invested in certain deals and still could not answer these questions. If you do not understand everything you can possibly understand about the prospect's decision criteria and process, you have no chance of influencing it when necessary. When working a long selling cycle involving multiple sales calls, keep an outline in your file called the Decision Matrix.

A Decision Matrix is a series of questions for which you need to have the answers. The matrix will help you understand everything you possibly can about the decision process. This tool should be used and developed throughout each new prospective account. For every person you contact in an organization, you need to develop a matrix of their individual decision criteria and the scope of their influence on the process.

> *The will to win is important. The will to prepare is vital.*
>
> — Joe Paterno

☞ DECISION MATRIX

The following is information you need to discover in order to understand and influence the prospect's decision process:

1. What has caused the prospect to look at changing vendors?
2. What is the date of implementation?
3. What is the date of decision?
4. What are the consequences associated with not solving the problem?
5. Will there be a test or production trial run?
6. Will the test or trial run happen before or after the decision on a vendor? Or, will you choose a vendor based on the results of a trial?
7. Has a test plan been developed?
8. What is the test plan?
9. Has the decision criteria been established? Or, will it be evolving and changing?
10. What's really going to drive this decision?
11. Who's really going to drive this decision? (Find the champion.)
12. Has the prospect ever faced a problem similar to this? Or, purchased products similar to mine? What criteria was used then?
13. Is there a committee?
14. What type of committee is it? Will the committee make the decision or are they simply the influencers?
15. Who are the members of the committee?
16. How is each committee member affected by the problem? Corporately affected or personally effected?

Exercise 6

Build a decision matrix for yourself. Think about the pertinent information you need to know for every deal that you work. Information about decision. The who's, what's, when's, why's and how's of a prospect's decision process. Most likely, you will not get all of the information that you want in your decision matrix on one sales call. Through the course of the sales cycle on any particular deal, you need to be conscious of these questions and constantly gathering information. You also need to ask the same question to numerous people throughout the corporate food chain to determine if the answers you are getting are consistent and valid.

☞ DECISION ZONE SUMMARY

Remember, our selling strategy is a series of rooms or zones, which we pass through in the course of our selling cycle—unlike the Problem Zone, which is more easily identified and which has clearly marked "boundaries." The Decision Zone can be more difficult to identify. Although there is a lot of work to do in this area, you will actually be gathering some of the information as you work your way through other zones. At some point in time during your selling cycle, you should feel you have completed this zone because you have gathered all of the information possible in order to understand and influence the prospect's decision process.

We can try to avoid making choices by doing nothing, but even that is a decision.
— Gary Collins

▨ ▨ ▨

MATCHING THE PROSPECT'S BUYING SYSTEM WITH YOUR SELLING STRATEGY

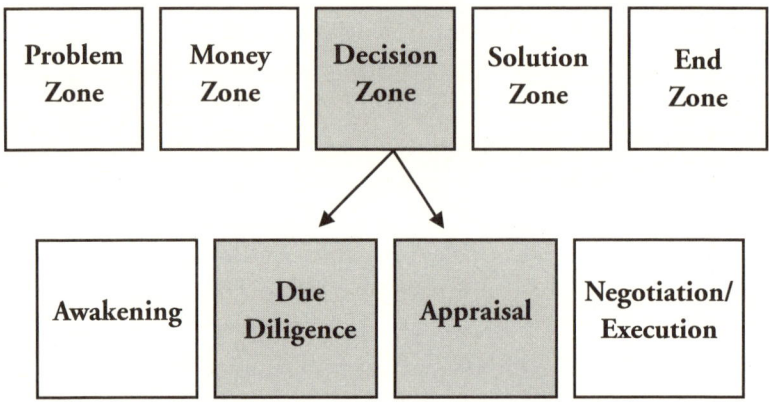

Your selling strategy dictates that you are working the Decision Zone at the same time that your prospect is in the Due Diligence and Appraisal stages.

Chapter 17
Solution Zone

Hence to fight and conquer in all your battles is not supreme excellence; supreme excellence consists in breaking the enemy's resistance without fighting.
— Sun Tzu, Chinese General

Once you thoroughly understand and have properly worked the Problem Zone, Money Zone and Decision Zone, you will begin moving to the Solution Zone. This is the time for you to make a presentation, prepare a proposal and/or submit a quotation for the appropriate products or services.

☞ COMMON MISTAKES IN THE SOLUTION ZONE

It is essential for you to remember your selling strategy and to move through each of these zones in the appropriate order. As I mentioned above, you must move through and understand each of the zones in your selling strategy in order to make the appropriate recommendations to your prospect in the Solution Zone. Too often, inexperienced or poorly skilled salespeople leap prematurely into presentation mode with their prospects. Frequently, this is done in an effort to create interest, extol the virtues of their features and benefits, or because the salesperson has bowed to the wishes of a prospect who has requested a presentation.

Premature presentation can damage your relationship with a prospective account on several levels:

1. It is impossible to make an appropriate presentation if you have not gathered the relevant information from the first three zones in your selling strategy. You cannot diagnose or fix a problem that you do not thoroughly understand. Therefore, you will not instill confidence in your prospect. In-

stead you will appear extremely unprofessional.

2. You will provide your prospect with free consulting by giving them information and possible solutions, which they can then use to prepare their decision criteria and shop your competition.

3. Without understanding the prospect's exact needs, you may give them ammunition to use later in the form of stalls and objections. Although your product or service may have ten value-added benefits, which could lead to a sale, your prospect may only have an interest in two of those issues. The other eight issues are icing on the cake, but are not relevant to their decision criteria. It is unwise to discuss irrelevant information. This will only prolong your sales cycle.

> *In the spider-web of facts, many a truth is strangled.*
>
> — Paul Eldridge

☞ SIMPLE RULES FOR THE SOLUTION ZONE

If you keep these few simple rules in mind, you will increase your chances of successfully crossing the Solution Zone:

1. Never give a presentation or prepare a proposal before you have gathered the necessary information.

2. Try not to make a presentation unless absolutely necessary, particularly if you feel it is too early in the sales process. Make it clear that you would not know what to present, since you don't thoroughly understand the problem(s). However, let the prospect know that you would be more than willing to make a presentation or submit a proposal, when you are totally comfortable that you understand the problems and needs.

3. Remember, the best presentation is the one you never have to make. If you have asked the right questions, if you understand the prospect's compelling reason for making the purchase, and if you have created sufficient trust and comfort with the prospect, there is a good chance you will not need to make a presentation at all. Even if you do, it may simply be a formality. Many sales can be made in the first three zones because the prospect consciously or subconsciously has already selected you as the preferred vendor.

4. Leverage the investment in your products or services vs. the cost of the problem remaining unsolved. One of the easiest sales to make is the one that demonstrates how much more expensive it will be.

5. Submit your proposal when the time is right. As I have mentioned before and will continue to do so . . . TIME KILLS DEALS. Don't submit your proposal until a definite timeline for decision has been established and the decision will happen very quickly once the proposal has been received.

> *In a hierarchy, every employee tends to rise to his level of incompetence.*
>
> — Laurence J. Peter

☞ A SOLUTION ZONE STORY

A few years ago, I was doing some consulting and training for a high tech company from Seattle. Their VP of Sales invited me to go to their Annual Sales Meeting in Las Vegas, which would be attended by their global sales force. In the typical fashion of most high tech corporations, the world sales meeting lasted about four days and had presentations from virtually every department in the company.

It was during the presentations by the Marketing Department that I witnessed first-hand how weak salespeople can be influenced by unnecessary information and poor advice. Both of these things can result in reduced profit margins and even in lost sales.

The Marketing Department had decided there were some key points that the sales force should convey to each and every prospect. For several hours, Marketing pounded on these poor, unsuspecting sales professionals that they had to carry forth the messages of: features and benefits; value propositions; exceptional service; and, most importantly, the company's commitment to research and development.

My client, the high tech company, spent a great deal of their annual budget on Research and Development. In fact, they were spending 25% of their budget in this area. Other companies in the industry were spending an average of 10% on Research and Development. Some companies were spending virtually nothing in this area. The Marketing Department decided that the company's vision for the future and their interest in developing new technology was an important message to carry forth to each and every prospect that the sales force came in contact with. Their company was continually breaking new ground. Who wouldn't be interested in learning more about their strong commitment to Research and Development?

As the Marketing presentation progressed, I found my stomach became increasingly tied in knots, my palms became sweaty and I came close to passing out from the throbbing pain shooting through my head. What were they thinking? All of these things were good . . . in the right context with the right prospect. However, there isn't one thing about any product or service which will be applicable to EVERY prospect.

About a month after the sales meeting, I was back in Seattle to continue my regular training sessions. It was then that I began talking with a mid-level sales manager who was extremely distressed and upset. It seemed that one of his salespeople had just missed out on a large deal, which he had come very close to winning. Quite accurately, this sales manager placed the blame on the Marketing Department.

The salesperson had worked his way through the entire process, had gathered volumes of information, understood all of the key players, devised a solution which would resolve all of their immediate issues and made his presentation in conjunction with submitting his proposal. As part of his presentation, the salesperson gave a brief history of the company, described their mission/vision and, following the instructions of the Marketing Department, hewent into great detail on the company's commitment to future Research and Development. He quantified this commitment by quoting the Marketing Department's figure that 25% of the annual budget went into this area.

Apparently, the message didn't resonate with that particular prospect—quite the opposite in fact. When the prospect responded to the proposal, they requested a 25% reduction in the price quoted and refused to move forward unless their wishes were met. They explained that they were not interested in funding future Research and Development. In fact, they were only interested in solving their current problem—PERIOD. Since 25% of my client's annual budget was spent on Research and Development, the prospect felt there was enough fat in the proposal to reduce the price. The prospect felt strongly about not being charged to fund future Research and Development. Needless to say, the salesperson couldn't get management to approve such a large reduction in price, and the sale never closed.

This is a prime example of providing the prospect with irrelevant and useless information, which came back to create a huge objection for the prospect. Stick to the facts, respond only to the compelling issues which the prospect is currently experiencing and refrain from offering any unnecessary information.

Features and benefits can damage your sale, if they are not relevant to your prospect's needs, and if you present them unnecessarily.

> *Success seems to be largely a matter of hanging on*
> *after others have let go.*
>
> — William Feather

MATCHING THE PROSPECT'S BUYING SYSTEM WITH YOUR SELLING STRATEGY

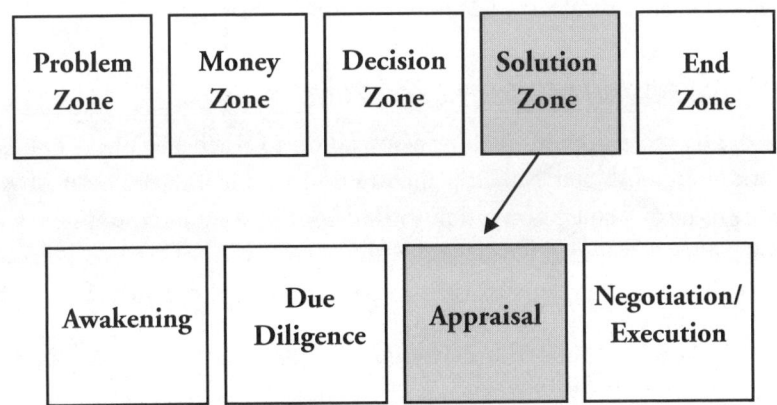

Your selling strategy dictates that when you are working the Solution Zone, the prospect is in the Appraisal stage.

CHAPTER 18

End Zone

Most people give up just when they're about to achieve success. They quit on the one yard line. They give up at the last minute of the game one foot from a winning touchdown.

— H. Ross Perot

Reaching the End Zone is the culmination of working all of the other zones in your selling strategy correctly. Obviously, this is when you will ask for the sale and the prospect will make a decision. Most of the time, this isn't a proactive zone because you have already properly worked the other four zones. Thus, the end zone becomes a natural occurrence.

☞ HOW DO YOU GET TO THE END ZONE

The most important thing you can do to reach the End Zone is to work to establish a crystal clear picture throughout the sales cycle of what happens next. Remember, you must find out the Why and the When. Control the process and the timeline to the best of your ability. As you work through the sales cycle with the prospect, continue to define the timeline and find out what the next step is.

Beware of Landmines

As you and the prospect negotiate to reach a final conclusion, you will be working to hammer out small details, which may seem much bigger than they really are. This would be a good time to refer back to Chapter 11, Negotiation and Execution in the Corporate Buying Cycle. Frequently, giving in to the prospect's will in order to close the sale may seem easier than negotiating the final conclusion. That's not negotiating . . . hold your ground.

It Ain't Over Till It's Over

Obviously, the best outcome is for the prospect to sign on the dotted line. Often, you will receive a "verbal" agreement with the promise of a signature pending "final" approval. The worst thing you can do at this point is to consider the sale final. After thanking the prospect for the order, you need to do two things:

1. Establish a definite timeline for final approval.

2. Ask the prospect what or who could derail the deal and keep the sale from closing.

If the prospect says that the deal is done, and nothing can derail it, you need to rephrase the question and ask again. Too often, someone or something lingering in the shadows will not come to light until the worst has already happened. If the prospect tells you there's a chance the sale could get derailed due to this, you will then be aware of what this is and can proactively address this with the right people. Get your biggest fear out on the table and address the issues. Don't ignore real stalls and objections.

☞ *IF THE WORST THING HAPPENS AND YOU DON'T GET THE SALE*

If the prospect chooses another vendor, don't give up. I am a firm believer that you can't lose what you never had AND that the promise of future business is not enough to make me walk away from the time I have already invested in the sales process. Therefore, give the prospect a grenade to deal with. Don't be afraid to bring up possible objections for the client to give your competition. Create questions, concerns and doubts about their vendor of choice. You've already been told no and, at this point, you have nothing to lose.

Date of Decision

Since you have been working to establish timelines and dates throughout the sales process, make sure to pinpoint the date that the final decision will be made. Once established, set a face-to-face appointment with the prospect either for the same day or as quickly after it as possible. Don't wimp out and don't let them off the hook. If you are going to be rejected, make them reject you in person. It will be much harder for them to do, and may work slightly in your favor.

As I stated in Chapter 13, A Selling Strategy, if you lose out on a sale, file an accident report. Analyze what went wrong, when it happened, why it happened and how you could have done things differently. The best thing to do at this point is to learn from your mistakes. The worst thing you can do is ignore the mistakes and repeat them again in the future.

> *The only real mistake is the one from which we learn nothing.*
> — John Powell

MATCHING THE PROSPECT'S BUYING SYSTEM WITH YOUR SELLING STRATEGY

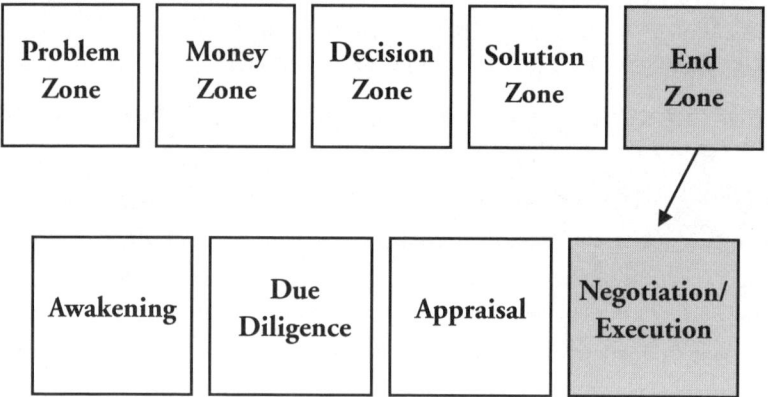

Your selling strategy dictates that when you are in the End Zone, the prospect should be in the Negotiation/Execution stage.

CHAPTER 19
Sales Tactics

There are many ways of going forward, but only one way of standing still.
— Franklin D. Roosevelt

A tactic can be defined as a skillful maneuver to achieve one's objectives. So, obviously, sales tactics are skillful maneuvers you use to help make your selling strategy successful. A strategy is a plan, but every good plan must have tactics in order to be effective. Occasionally, some selling professionals have a strategy, but I've met very few selling professionals who were tactical before I trained them.

Understanding and using sales tactics is a powerful tool. In my own personal sales endeavors, the use of certain tactics at the right time has completely turned a negative situation into a positive situation. The tactics that I am about to introduce to you can be used anywhere and everywhere in your selling cycle or your selling strategy (zones). Just understanding these tactics is not enough. You must practice using them. Several good places to practice are at home, in your social life and at the office with co-workers. Before you use these tactics in a game (sales call), keep them on the practice field until they are second nature.

Don't be afraid to take a big step. You can't cross a chasm in two small jumps.
— David Llyod George

☞ SALES TACTIC # 1: MUTUAL AGREEMENT

A mutual agreement is when you get your prospect to agree to something at some future point in time. I'm going to say it again . . . when you get your prospect to agree to something at some future point in time. That "something" could be anything—a very large issue or a very small issue. The future point in time could be ten minutes from now or six weeks from now. For example, let's assume on a sales call, towards the beginning of the meeting, you say to your prospect, "Ellen, would this be fair? At the end of this meeting, we could discover that my products and services may not make sense for you at this point in time. Therefore, it's safe to assume there's no reason for us to have another meeting. On the other hand, if we discover that it may be valuable for us to meet again, could we schedule the next meeting before I leave?"

You have just set a mutual agreement with your prospect. The something (issue) is a second meeting, and the future point in time is at the end of our current meeting.

What did this mutual agreement achieve for you? First of all, it provided a crystal clear understanding of what happens next. The opposite of crystal clear is mutual mystification—where neither party fully understands what happens next. It also became a time saving tool for you; this will keep the selling cycle moving forward. You're not going to be playing phone tag with Ellen in order to schedule a second meeting, nor will you be left wondering if a second meeting will occur. At the end of the first meeting, you will have enforced the mutual agreement by asking if there was a reason to get back together. The answer was yes. So, you set the meeting.

Another benefit of using mutual agreements is that you are getting your prospect in the habit of working with you and agreeing with you. Throughout your selling cycle, your prospect will become comfortable with your style of mutual agreements which create a crystal clear understanding. Mutual agreements also defuse future stalls and objections.

How to Set and Use Mutual Agreements

When setting a mutual agreement, the proper verbiage to use is: "Would this be fair," "Would this be reasonable," "Would this make sense," or "Would this be agreeable." Then you propose the mutual agreement, which again is getting them to agree to something at some future point in time.

When the time comes to fulfill the mutual agreement, you must remind or enforce the mutual agreement with your prospect. You need to let them know that there was an agreement in place and they should honor that agreement.

☞ SALES TACTIC # 2: OK NOT OK

It is human nature when someone is too OK that they make the people around them not OK. News reports, soap operas, combative afternoon TV talk shows and gossip publications all have one thing in common—they show us human situations which are not OK. Therefore, we instinctively feel better about our own lives and personal situations.

Somewhere in the past, you probably had a sales manager, or you went through Sales Training 101 which instructed you to be strong and confident in front of your prospects. This can create a big problem if you're too strong, too confident and too dominant in front of your prospects. If you are too OK, your prospect may become not OK. If your prospect is not OK, you are reducing your chances of doing business with them. The goal is for your prospect to be OK. Therefore, it is absolutely tactical for you to be a little unsure of yourself or to act a little bit confused—especially in the Problem Zone. By doing this, you are making your prospect OK. When they are OK, they will give you valuable information in an unguarded manner. Now, don't go overboard and act like a complete goof. In a subtle manner, act like you're the student and they're the teacher.

☞ SALES TACTIC # 3: ROTATION

Rotation is when your prospect asks you a question, you ignore their question and don't answer it. Rather, you respond to them by asking them a question. For example:

Prospect: "How many of these systems have you sold?"

Salesperson: "Apparently, the number of systems we've sold is an important issue to you?"

Prospect: "Well, it could be."

Salesperson: "Could you share those thoughts with me?"

I'm not suggesting you rotate every question a prospect asks you. However, I am suggesting you rotate questions that: A) you don't really know the answer to; or, B) you don't know why they're asking the question. If you don't know why they're asking the question, never assume.

Let's stay with this example question and pretend that you answer it:

Prospect: "How many of these systems have you sold?"

Salesperson: "We have sold thousands of these systems throughout the world."

Prospect: "We're not interested in a system which is this widely used. We're hoping to use a system that is somewhat unknown and almost appears to be proprietary or unique to our company—something which sets us apart."

So, the salesperson assumed the prospect would take great comfort in the fact that there were so many of these systems in the marketplace. In reality, that was not the case. By not answering the question and rotating, the salesperson would have gathered enough information to answer the question in a much more soothing manner. By rotating, the salesperson may have eventually answered the question like this:

Salesperson: "We have numerous systems installed throughout the world. However, most of these systems have not been customized. We are capable of customizing this system to give your company a unique product which will appear to be proprietary."

When Rotating

When you rotate, 90% of the time the prospect will not catch or pick up on the rotation. They most likely will answer your question and not be at all consumed that you did not answer theirs. When rotating, your tonality must be soothing and nurturing. If you appear to be glib or sarcastic in any way, the client will definitely pick up on your tone and notice that you did not answer the question. A rule of thumb, if they caught your rotation and re-ask the question, you will probably have to answer it—even though you're not prepared to answer it.

It is almost impossible to develop the tactical sales skill of rotating if you don't consciously practice it and perfect it before you use it on sales calls.

☞ SALES TACTIC # 4: TENTATIVE MANEUVERING

This is the art of phrasing questions, statements, responses or opinions in more of a tentative manner than a positive manner. Being too positive can make your prospect not OK. Tentative maneuvering can defuse the combative attitudes that prospects sometimes have. For example:

Wrong: "My company is the market leader."
Right: "Working with the market leader may not be important to you."

Wrong: "I'm extremely confident we can provide a solution for you."
Right: "At this point, I don't know if our solution is perfect for you."

Wrong: "I can provide you with numerous referrals and references."

Right: "Sure, I can provide you with referrals and they will tell you wonderful things about me and my company. However, I'm unsure that their situations will be relevant to your issues."

Purpose of Tentative Maneuvering

If you can get the hang of phrasing things in more of a tentative than a positive manner, you stand a better chance that your prospects will convince *themselves* rather than *you* trying to convince *them*. It is very hard to convince anybody of anything. It's much easier to use the right phraseology which enables them to draw their own conclusions and convince themselves. Although it may be referred to in different terminology, tentative maneuvering is a tactic which is widely used by psychiatrists. They rarely, if ever, tell their patients what the heck is wrong with them. Instead, they will use a lot of tentative maneuvering so the patient identifies the problem on their own.

☞ SALES TACTIC # 5: FUTURE TO PRESENT

This tactic is when you take your prospect into the future (so they have a vision of the future), then bring them back to the present. For example:

Salesperson: "Joe, let's pretend for just a moment that this current situation or problem is still with you six months or a year from now. Can you explain to me what that will mean for your business?"

Prospects, like all people, exercise denial. If you take them out into the future, and let them discover on their own the consequences of not fixing a problem, you are helping them confront their denial, form a greater sense of urgency, and you will advance or speed up the selling cycle.

The phraseology or verbiage you use when doing future to present is: "Let's pretend," "Let's imagine," "Can you paint a picture for me or if you had a crystal ball." Then, take them into the future so they can understand the consequences and bring them back to the present to deal with them.

☞ SALES TACTIC # 6: THE ONE-LINER

Have you ever been caught in a situation where your prospect says something unexpectedly which absolutely drops you to your knees? You weren't ready for it. You didn't expect it. Thus, you're paralyzed and you don't know how to deal with it on the spot. As a result, you start talking to yourself, "Oh no! I can't believe he said that. Holy cow! How am I going to deal with this? What in the heck do I do now?"

You're having a crisis conversation with yourself and the prospect has "gotcha" and they know it. Therefore, it's important for you to have a one-liner—a statement or question that rolls out of your mouth to keep you from talking to yourself and puts the ball back in their court for further explanation. Here is the one-liner:

If you need to respond to a statement: "You must be telling me this for a reason."

If you need to respond to a question: "You must be asking me this for a reason."

This one-liner is bullet-proof. It doesn't matter what is said to you, this response will always apply, and will not be out of context or sequence. When caught off-guard, use the one-liner. Then, shut up, don't say anything else and let the prospect respond. The prospect may be Cool Hand Luke and simply respond, "I am." Then, your next question is, "Could you please explain? Tell me more." Again, shut up, listen and let the prospect talk.

It's possible what the prospect has to say will be the most important things you need to know in order to make a sale. It's possible there are issues, or stalls and objections, which you haven't discovered or dealt with yet. It's also possible this is the negotiation hammer, which the prospect is using to get greater concessions from you. Blind-siding and paralyzing a salesperson are powerful tactics for prospects.

The one-liner has given you time and space to recover from the emotional blow you have been dealt. You can now sit back, listen and determine whether the issue is serious, or if it's just smoke and mirrors to keep you off-guard and willing to make greater concessions.

> *We are what we repeatedly do. Excellence, then, is not an act, but a habit.*
>
> — Aristotle

☞ SALES TACTICS SUMMARY

If you've ever been enrolled in my training program, you know there are several other tactics, which I have not mentioned in this section. These six tactics are more than enough for you to try to master right now. It wouldn't be prudent to put more food on your plate than what you can eat.

In Chapter 12, Happy Hunting/Prospecting, I promised to help you develop a good thirty-second commercial in this chapter, Sales Tactics. Now that you understand these tactics, a good thirty-second commercial will make more sense to you.

☞ THE THIRTY-SECOND COMMERCIAL

Here's my thirty-second commercial that I use when prospecting. Remember, I sell consulting and training services to corporations. My entry into a corporation is usually in the sales department. Thus, I call on CEOs, VPs of Sales and Regional or District Sales Managers. So, let's pretend I'm making a phone call to try to get an appointment with Dan Carrell, VP of Sales at XYZ Company.

Ring, ring, ring.

Me: Is Dan in?

Dan: Yes. This is Dan.

Me: Mr. Carrell, my name is Mark McGlinchey. I'm a salesperson which means you probably want to hang up on me or don't have thirty seconds to talk to me.

Dan: I've got thirty seconds.

Me: Great. Would this be acceptable? I'll do a thrity-second commercial and at the end of the commercial, you can decide if there's any value in continuing the conversation. And, if not, I certainly won't bother you any further.

Dan: Yes. Go ahead.

Me: My company, the McGlinchey Group, works with companies like yours to help improve the productivity and skills of your sales force through better methods of evaluating, hiring and training sales professionals. Most of my clients use my services for one of the three following reasons:

1. The sales force is not developing enough new business or their prospecting skills are not what they should be.

2. The sales force is not doing a good enough job holding their margins which can be affecting the company's bottom line.

3. Too many deals are staying in the pipeline way too long rather than closing in a timely fashion.

You may not have any of these concerns.

Dan: No. Actually I do.

Me: Dan, my thirty-second commercial is up. But since sales is my profession, I would love to hear your feedback.

Dan: Well, actually Mark, all three of the issues you brought up are issues here at XYZ. However, ongoing new business and new accounts is an issue we're very concerned about.

Me: Tell me more.

Dan: Blah, blah, blah. Blah, blah, blah. Blah, blah, blah. On an on. (The more Dan talks about it, the more he will feel the problem.)

Me: Dan, I can't promise you that I have a magic solution, but this is my area of expertise. Would it make sense for you to invite me in for an hour to continue this conversation?

☞ ANALYZING THE THIRTY-SECOND COMMERCIAL AND TACTICS

Mutual Agreements

I did it twice in this thirty-second commercial. The first one was, "Would this be acceptable? I'll do a thirty-second commercial and at the end of the commercial, you can decide if there's any value in continuing the conversation. And, if not, I certainly won't bother you any further." The second one was, "Dan, my thirty-second commercial is up. But since sales is my profession, I would love to hear your feedback."

OK not OK

I used this tactic when I said, "Mr. Carrell, my name is Mark McGlinchey. I'm a salesperson which means you probably want to hang up on me or don't have thirty seconds to talk to me." I was not OK and since I was not OK, Dan was OK and he rescued me by allowing me thirty seconds.

Tentative Maneuvering

I used what I consider to be a three-hook tentative maneuver. I threw out three common issues that almost any VP of Sales should be or is concerned with. Then, I followed it up with a classical tentative maneuver statement or question. "You may not have any of these concerns."

Now, think about this for just a minute. Instead of phrasing this as "You may not have any of these concerns," I could have phrased it more positive than tentative and said, "You probably have one of these concerns." Most likely, Dan would have responded to me by saying, "No. Not really." And, I would have been dead in the saddle. By phrasing it in a tentative manner, I relaxed him and enabled him to respond to me in the manner I was hoping for.

☞ FURTHER ANALYSIS

The way that I did this commercial put Dan in a position that there were only five ways he could respond to me:

1. "Yes. I am concerned about # 1 (new business)."
2. "Yes. I am concerned about # 2 (shrinking margins)."
3. "Yes. I am concerned about # 3 (deals taking too long to close)."
4. "No. I'm really not concerned about these three issues. However, I am concerned about XXX."

Any of these first four responses will continue to keep me in the ballgame to possibly get an appointment with Dan to discuss these issues, find and intensify compelling problems and create an Awakening with Dan.

5. "You're right, Mark. None of these issues are a concern for me." Now, my response will be, "I thought that would be the case. Dan, as it pertains to your sales force, are there any issues now, or any issues that may come into play in the future (I just used *future to present*), which could concern you?" His answer could be no, which means I will probably not get an appointment with him. Or, his answer could be discussing a possible issue, which means I'm still in the ballgame and it's possible for me to get an appointment with him.

Exercise 7

Write a thirty-second commercial for your-self. Remember, a thirty-second commercial is to be mainly used via the telephone to intro-duce yourself and to try to set an appointment with a prospect. Once you are happy with the thirty-second commercial you have put to-gether, you should use it and repeat it on an ongoing basis. It should become second nature to you.

Make your commercial tactical by reviewing and using the tactics presented to you in this chapter. The commercial should produce XX number of responses from your prospect. You should know exactly how you will handle each possible response the prospect may give you.

SUMMARY OF PART THREE
Managing the Selling Cycle: Huddle Up! We've Got the Ball Now!

The past eight chapters have been about you—the sales professional—controlling your selling cycle. You cannot control chaos. Without a selling strategy, which you repeat on an ongoing basis, you're winging it. Thus, the prospects will not only control their buying cycle, they will also control your selling process.

The selling zone method is a strategy you can put into use. Realize that a sales cycle can and should be divided into certain zones. Each zone has a purpose, each zone provides objectives, which you are trying to accomplish. Of course, every good strategy must have tactics. Tactics are the fuel that the strategy runs on. New strategies and tactics cannot be mastered overnight. Rather, they are developed over time and with practice. If you use this selling strategy along with the tactics that I have provided, professional selling will not only become easier but will also be more enjoyable.

If you're in sales, you have now finished this book. However, if you are in sales management or aspire to be in sales management, I suggest you continue and read the next section.

> The harder the conflict, the more glorious the triumph. What we obtain too cheap, we esteem too lightly; it is dearness only that gives everything its value. I love the man that can smile in trouble, that can gather strength from distress and grow brave by reflection. 'Tis the business of little minds to shrink; but he whose heart is firm, and whose conscience approves his conduct, will pursue his principles unto death.
>
> — Thomas Paine

PART FOUR

SALES MANAGER'S HANDBOOK:

Six Principles of Sales Management

CHAPTER 20
Finding & Interviewing Candidates

*It is no use saying, "We are doing our best." You
have got to succeed in doing what is necessary.*
— Sir Winston Churchill

I can't imagine a more challenging task than managing salespeople or a sales force. When I think of sales management, I envision a town like Dodge City in the 1860s where the sheriff is the sales manager and his sales force is made up of all the rowdy cowboys who he needs to keep in line. This imagery of sales management may not always be accurate; however, there is little doubt that it is sometimes challenging and, at times, it can be quite stressful.

If you are a VP of Sales, a Regional or District Sales Manager, or have the responsibility of managing and guiding salespeople, the following chapters should provide some useful information and insightful guidance. There is no doubt a complete book can be written and dedicated to sales management, but it's my style to keep things simple. Therefore, I'm not going to give you a step-by-step guide on how to micromanage a sales force. Rather, I will provide you with six principles to employ as part of your management strategy.

☞ FINDING & INTERVIEWING CANDIDATES

There are over 25,000,000 selling professionals in the United States. Almost 40% of them change jobs on an annual basis. That's right! Data provided by the U. S. Bureau of Labor and Statistics indicates that a typical business will experience a turnover of almost 40% of their sales force annually. We could list many reasons as to why this rate is so high, and some of the many reasons have validity. However, in my opinion, the biggest factor in sales force turnover is one reason . . . *most salespeople are not very good.* Thus, they're chased out the door, or they get out the door themselves before the guillotine falls on them.

The formula for developing a great sales force is 40% hiring, 40% good skills training and 20% management. Therefore, finding and interviewing candidates correctly is of utmost importance.

☛ *THE RIGHT SOURCES*

There are a zillion different publications—both print and Internet—where you can place an ad when you want to fill a sales position. Most companies have a "herd mentality" and like to use the biggest or most popular sources. There are two very large Internet sources that come to mind (I'm sure you know who I am referring to). In the past few years, the Internet has certainly become the most efficient and economical way to place a want ad and, personally, I feel the Internet is a better tool than placing an ad in print publications. The problem with these two giant Internet boards and other large Internet sources is that they have turned into a haven for job hoppers.

These sites are the greatest and easiest tools a vagabond salesperson has ever had at their disposal. For the most part, the salespeople you find on these super-large Internet sites are not the people you want to be finding. I prefer to find a passive/active candidate, rather than a totally active candidate. A passive/active candidate is someone who doesn't really consider themselves in the open job market. But rather, these individuals keep their ear to the ground and brush up their resume if they come across or hear about a better opportunity.

To find passive/active candidates, you need to place your want ads on smaller, boutique websites, such as industry specific sites, industry newsletters, organization sites or targeted geographic sites. Sites where the aggressive and progressive industry sales rep may go for reasons other than simply to look at want ad. However, while they are there, they may notice the want ads. You're not looking for a flock of sparrows. You're looking for an eagle and, often, they fly alone. So, try to figure out the website in your industry where the eagles may be visiting.

☞ HOW TO WRITE AN AD

There is an art and a science to writing the proper want ad. Don't leave it up to your HR Department to write the ad. Human Resource Departments understand sales and salespeople about as much as we understand brain surgery.

The wrong ad will over-emphasize the company's vision, the super benefit package, corporate culture, work environment and being a part of a team. All of the things that a wimpy salesperson, who is looking for a place to hide, will love.

The right ad may include a handsome benefit package. However, the overriding message in the ad will be money, compensation, commissions and forging your own destiny. Also, the right ad will state that you are looking for a hunter or a prospector to develop new accounts and new business. That statement is sure to chase away all of the wimps' resumes, which you do not want to waste your time reviewing. The purpose of good ad writing is not to get 200 responses to find one or two decent candidates; but rather, ten to a dozen responses with over half of the candidates having the right stuff.

☞ MCGLINCHEY GROUP

Sorry about the advertisement here . . . but now a word from our sponsor.

My company has developed a process to help our clients find and qualify only the best sales professionals. We have an eight step process:

1. Research and evaluate alternative job posting sites and select the right sites for each of your job openings.

2. Create a powerful, persuasive job posting that will attract both active and passive candidates.

3. Perform the time consuming task of posting your job to multiple websites.

4. Electronically capture and process candidate resumes received over the Internet, via fax and through the mail.

5. Pre-screen resumes and eliminate those which are not acceptable to your designated candidate criteria.

6. Present a final slate of qualified, interested candidates.

7. Enhance your corporate image with timely responses to interested candidates.

8. Consolidate billing from all sites and present a single invoice.

Therefore, if you have a need, we can certainly help you as well. With our assistance, all you will have to do is interview and hire. Contact us at www.mcglincheygroup.com.

☞ *INTERVIEWING*

When interviewing prospective sales professionals, your interviewing process needs to be both strategic and tactical. Thus, you have a plan and method to achieve that plan. Too often, sales managers make the mistake of trying to sell the candidate on the opportunity. Therefore, the interviewing process takes almost a reverse twist. The sales manager may be trying to convince the candidate to take the opportunity, rather than the candidate convincing the sales manager that they are the right person for the job.

Avoid some of the common mistakes of talking too much, explaining too much, extolling the virtues of the company and hyping the opportunity.

> *The true test of character is not how much we know how to do, but how we behave when we don't know what to do.*
>
> — John Holt

The Right Interview

Especially in the first interview, your strategy should be to make the candidate uncomfortable. You need to pretend that you are the hardest prospect they have ever made a sales call on. If they can't handle themselves under fire in this situation, doesn't it make sense that they won't be able to handle themselves under fire in front of a prospect? Keep these tactics in mind when interviewing candidates:

1. Your general demeanor should be short, curt and somewhat unfriendly. What you are trying to learn from this is: does he or she become emotionally involved too quickly on a sales call, and can he or she fight through a tough situation to establish bonding and rapport.

2. You want to ask him or her personal questions about money, such as: "I like your tie or I like your suit. How much did that cost?" "What kind of car are you driving? How much did that cost?" These types of questions will enable you to discover how comfortable or uncomfortable the candidate is discussing money. Great salespeople are generally comfortable talking about money.

3. Ask the candidate what his or her income has been for the past five years. You're trying to discover the comfort zone. By comparing your compensation plan to the candidate's comfort zone, you should get an idea of how that person will perform.

4. Ask the candidate numerous questions about prospecting. "How do you prospect? How much time per day do you spend prospecting? What methods do you use to prospect?" If the candidate seems at all stumped, he or she probably does not prospect. If the candidate tells you he or she spends more than three hours a day prospecting, that person is most likely lying and probably rarely prospects. Otherwise, he or she would realize that spending three hours a day prospecting is almost impossible and is hard to achieve in most industries. If the candidate uses words like "networking" and "marketing," or tells you he or she likes to send out letters or use e-mail, this candidate is certainly not a hunter. Great hunters and prospectors consider the telephone the only realistic method of prospecting. If a candidate is scared of the phone, don't hire that person.

5. Ask the candidate about his or her professional and life goals. If the answer is in great detail then most likely he or she does have goals. If the answers are short and the candidates wants to change the subject, he or she probably doesn't have goals or a destination. Lack of destination causes a lack of desire.

6. Ask the candidate what his or her five largest sales were during the past year. The candidate should be able to rattle these off without a problem. If he or she hedges, stalls or seems uncomfortable, it's a sure sign that he or she has not been able to produce in the past.

If your demeanor is tough and your questions are probing, you're going to know after one interview if you have a candidate who not only *can* sell but *will* sell. I believe only 20% of salespeople are worth hiring. Therefore, four out of five salespeople should be flunking this type of an interview and it should be obvious which ones fail. With the candidate who you do like, you will need to repair some of the damage done in the interview. You shouldn't care if the other candidates thought you were a jerk—it doesn't matter. However, with the one candidate you would like to interview again and possibly hire, you need to change your tone and establish bonding and rapport during the last five minutes of the interview. This should be done just in case you were so good on your side of the interview that you might have chased that candidate off.

> *Character cannot be developed in ease and quiet.*
> *Only through experience of trial and suffering can*
> *the soul be strengthened, ambition inspired, and*
> *success achieved.*
>
> — Helen Keller

Exercise 8

Devise a list of questions to be used in an interview to uncover a candidate's strengths and weaknesses pertaining to the 7 Building Blocks.

Review the first six chapters on Self-Improvement and the Building Blocks in the first section of this book. These are the things you want to discover during the interviewing process, since these are the things which are hardest to change and hardest to train. Understanding the buying cycle and having a selling strategy with tactics is the 40% which can be trained.

CHAPTER 21
Evaluating & Hiring Candidates

*Good leaders make people feel that they're at the
very heart of things, not at the periphery. Everyone
feels that he or she makes a difference to the success
of the organization. When that happens people
feel centered and that gives their work meaning.*
— Warren Bennis

When evaluating and hiring sales professionals, you need to prioritize what the top criteria is that you are looking for. When I am involved in the process of hiring sales professionals there are obvious qualities that I look for, such as:

1. Does the candidate look professional?

2. Do the candidate have an adequate command of the English language?

3. Does the candidate have industry knowledge and experience?

4. It's a bonus if the candidate has a rolodex or accounts which he or she can immediately start calling on after taking a new position.

5. Does the candidate have a selling strategy and tactics? Candidates rarely do have sound strategies and tactics.

However, there is one thing that I'm always looking for. The one thing which is toughest to train. The one thing which 10-20% of all salespeople have. That one thing is . . . the ability to be a hunter.

I'm not interested in hiring farmers—nor should you be. Farmers are a dime a dozen, their scope is limited and their up-side has a ceiling. Generally, farmers are poor hunters. On the other hand, hunters can adequately farm when necessary. My first method for trying to determine whether or not a candidate is a hunter is a good solid interviewing process with probing questions (detailed in the last chapter). If a candidate survives the interview process, and I think I have a hunter on my hands (a person who will prospect and who has prospected in the past), I want to formally test that candidate, and administer some sort of evaluation to validate my hunch.

> *You can't build a reputation on what you're going to do.*
>
> — Henry Ford

☞ TESTS AND EVALUATIONS

If you go to the Internet and type in a search for sales tests and evaluations, you will see that there are close to one hundred sales tests or evaluations that have been developed. These tests were designed to help employers make determinations about sales candidates.

The type of tests or evaluations that I prefer will tell me more about the personal makeup of a sales candidate rather than that candidate's skill sets. It's a lot easier to change someone's skills than it is to change someone's personal makeup. There are two or three tests out there that I refer to as the four squares evaluations. These tests break people down into one of four categories (refer to Chapter 12.) True hunters always come out of the same category—the D category—dominant or driver. If a person comes out of a category other than the D category, they can certainly be trained to hunt, but they're not built for hunting. Baggage, head trash and life scripting will get in their way.

☞ AN EVALUATION STORY

In 1998, I began working with the regional office of a large telecommunications company that sold both telephone service and Internet access. My consulting services were not being used company-wide, but rather one of their Regional Sales Managers invested in my services. Most people would consider the sales jobs within this company to be "churn and burn" jobs—meaning the stress level of the job was so great that high turnover was expected and certainly had been the company's history.

This region was experiencing 80% annual turnover of its sales force. However, the 20% that did not turnover were all earning well into six-figures. Naturally, when 80% of the sales force is turning over, sales management positions are also turning over at a rapid rate. This is primarily due to the workload and stress placed on the managers. This company needed to hire true hunters—and only true hunters. Hunters were the only type of sales professionals who could survive and thrive in this environment.

I chose a testing and evaluation product that this region began to employ as part of their hiring process. The first thing we did was test all of the salespeople in the region with longevity—those people who had survived and were doing well. By doing this, we were able to devise a control standard. From this standard, it was decided we would not hire a sales candidate unless that candidate scored in a certain range. Anyone who scored outside that range would not be hired—even if management had a good gut feeling that the person would work out. Within a year's time, turnover in this region was reduced from 80% to 30%. Naturally, less turnover usually means more profitability and a better environment for both salespeople and sales managers.

☞ BEFORE HIRING

If a candidate has come through the interviewing, testing and evaluation processes, two last steps should be taken before an offer is given. The first is a background check. Usually, a good background check will cost in the range of $200 to $350. Since 9-11-01, we should all do our part to help secure our nation and our employer. Obviously, a background check can provide confirming or non-confirming information about a person other than their origin or nationality.

The second step is that we should insist that the candidate give us two or three client or customer referrals. We should talk to the people they have been selling to. A sales candidate may fight you on this one and tell you this is endangering their current position. No, it isn't. You can't fire someone for interviewing with another company. There are laws against that. There's two things I'm trying to discover by asking for client referrals. First, does this candidate have some clients who will speak highly of him or her. And, secondly, if the candidate is really opposed to this, it raises a red flag. At this point, if you're asking for a client referral, it is probably your last requirement before extending an offer. If the sales candidate knows this, and wants to accept your offer, this should not be a problem for the candidate.

CHAPTER 22
Manage—Don't Babysit

The important thing to recognize is that it takes a team, and the team ought to get credit for the wins and the losses. Successes have many fathers, failures have none.

— Philip Caldwell

Your role is to be a manager of selling professionals. Your responsibilities are to lead and guide your sales force, and to produce revenue for your company. It is not your duty to babysit the sales force. Therefore, you need to delegate responsibilities. Since you can't possibly achieve everything yourself, delegation is the only way to effectively work and hit your company's targets.

In addition to freeing up valuable time for the sales manager, delegation permits members of your team to develop their own leadership capabilities.

☞ DEVELOP DECISION MAKERS

By involving these individuals in the decision-making process, the people who are nearest to the situation will be allowed to voice their opinions and feel that they are an integral part of the process.

☞ DEVELOP ACCOUNTABILITY

In conjunction with delegation, members of your team will become accountable for achieving goals and their portions of the overall strategic plan. Success and failure can both be recognized and dealt with accordingly.

☞ DEVELOP LEADERS

Within your own team, individuals can be groomed to assume additional responsibilities. Over time, these individuals can become easier to promote. In addition, individuals who feel they are an integral part of the team and its process will become more loyal in the long run.

☞ IMPROVE MOTIVATION

With additional responsibility employees will inherently feel more invested in the overall productivity and success of the company. The results will directly reflect his or her own work ethic, abilities and success. Therefore, there will be additional motivation to succeed.

☞ IMPROVE MORALE

In addition to motivation, an improvement in morale is a direct result of distributing additional responsibilities. Team members who truly feel needed and that they are making a contribution will create a more positive atmosphere for the people around them.

☞ MEETING MANAGEMENT

Obviously, the proper amount of time or days must be set aside for quarterly sales meetings or annual sales meetings. However, one of the biggest misuses of time occurs in non-productive and disorganized daily or weekly meetings. Managers can get caught in a trap of spending too much time in unnecessary or poorly planned meetings.

Try to insure that weekly sales meetings last only a half an hour, and unscheduled or impromptu meetings last fifteen minutes or less. Establish the following rules for these meetings:

1. There is no good news or bad news—just information and updates.
2. Always have an agenda—and stick to it!
3. Eliminate unnecessary meetings.
4. Only have meetings to make decisions.
5. Never invite people just to be polite.
6. Don't ignore a tough issue.

☞ USE EXPERTS

You were hired to manage salespeople and to manage sales revenue. As mentioned before, you were not hired to be a babysitter. Now, get your seatbelt on! You were also not hired to be a trainer. It's acceptable in a very small company that you may have to train salespeople on the products or procedures. However, in larger companies, this is a complete misuse of your time. When you were a salesperson, you were probably pretty good. That's why you were promoted into sales management. Most likely, you have what I call "non-transferable" skills. Meaning, you really can't teach what you did successfully in sales. Be willing to hire outside expertise to train your sales force in the areas of strategies, tactics and skills. It's usually a very high return on investment.

> *Winning is not a sometime thing; it's an all time thing. You don't win once in a while, you don't do things right once in a while, you do them right all the time. Winning is habit. Unfortunately, so is losing.*
>
> — Vince Lombardi

☞ WINNER / LOSER PROFILES

One of the most valuable roles you can play as a sales manager is to be an analyst and to guide your sales force with the vast knowledge you have acquired analytically. Develop what I call a winner/loser profile. This is a matrix or graph to help you and your sales force understand and recognize the traits of a successful deal vs. an unsuccessful deal.

Objectives for Identifying Winners and Losers

1. Realistic assessment of future business.
2. Provides base for development of strategy.
3. Highlights type of business we should try to develop.
4. Understanding current standing gives us the best chance to make meaningful change.

Characterization of Successful Deals

Have each selling professional you manage characterize their last three to five successful deals, according to:

1. Size of order.
2. Size of the prospect.
3. Individuals involved in the decision.
4. Level of individuals involved in the decision.
5. Departments involved.
6. Product being considered.
7. RFP or RFI.
8. Committee decision.
9. Budget / non-budgeted.
10. Length of cycle.
11. Competitor involvement.
12. Members of our team.
13. Miscellaneous factors.

Characterization of Unsuccessful Deals

Repeat the same procedures used for successful deals.

Exercise 9

Build a graph of the elements that you feel are needed to analyze in order to develop a winner/loser profile. Then, teach your sales force to do the same. When you have completed this exercise, I think you will find it both interesting and amazing that there are common threads which always indicate a winning deal and common threads which usually indicate a deal you have lost.

By developing a winner/loser profile in matrix or graph form, it should help you and your sales force will realize that there are some common denominators in deals you usually win vs. deals you are not winning. When you find these common denominators on winning deals, your strategy should be to keep doing what's been successful and do more of it, and don't make many changes.

Your strategy on deals which fall into the loser profile should be to do something different, call at higher levels, limit the amount of time you will work on these deals and have your sales professionals always "going for no"—meaning, they're always challenging the prospect to cut them loose and tell them goodbye. Developing a winner/loser profile for each salesperson you manage keeps you managing rather than babysitting.

CHAPTER 23

Stop Rescuing Your Salespeople

The ultimate leader is one who is willing to develop people to the point that they eventually surpass him or her in knowledge and ability.
— Fred A. Manske, Jr.

☛ LET THEM WIN AND LOSE ALONE

Many sales managers believe their number one responsibility is to help their salespeople close deals. As if their salesperson has pitched seven innings of a nine inning game, now it's time for the sales manager to come in and close the deal. It's human nature to want to help or rescue the sales professionals you manage. If you're a sales manager, chances are good that some, if not all, of your compensation is based on results. Therefore, if one of your people is working a deal, you want to pitch in and help.

It's also possible that your boss or people above you in the corporate food chain see it as your responsibility to help your salespeople close deals. One, two, three . . . take a deep breath and STOP! Your salespeople have to learn to win or lose alone and must continue to win or lose alone.

Two bad things are happening if you continue to rescue your salespeople:

1. The salespeople become much too dependant on you. Somewhere down the road, there may not be enough of you to go around. This process also hampers their skill development. This practice also short-circuits their confidence in themselves.

2. You will be credited with all losses and never recognized in the corporation for a win. This will work at both ends of the scale. The people

above you in the food chain will feel this way and the people you manage will also feel this way. Since you are involved in the losses, and your presence is considered to be a reason for the loss, poor salespeople now get a longer tenure. If it wasn't for you, they would have been more successful.

Actively working deals with your salespeople puts you in a position where you are enabling rather than managing. It's perfectly fine to debrief them about any deals that they are working, or to give suggestions and advice about those deals. However, do not work the deal with them. If you have to help any salesperson work deals, you either need to fire that person or put him or her in a good skills training program.

☞ MANAGE BEHAVIOR

Manage the behavior and activities of your salespeople—do not try to manage their skills and strategies. Hopefully, your salespeople have a destination with a roadmap and a compass. If they don't, you certainly need to provide the road map and a compass—which is mandatory, above the trouble line activity that you expect them to be accomplishing (refer to Chapter 5). Sales may not happen if you try to manage results. However, results happen much more frequently if you are managing behavior and activity.

☞ MANAGE THE PIPELINE

This concept is very similar to managing behavior and activity. Chances are that you have quarterly numbers, which you need to meet. You should know the average length of time in your selling cycle or the selling cycle of your salespeople. You should have a good handle on what percentage of business usually closes in comparison to the deals which are being worked. Let's pretend you have a quota next quarter for $10 million in new business, the sales cycle is about ninety days long, and the typical closing rate of your sales force is 30%. Thus, by doing the math, it's pretty obvious you need $30 million in the pipeline at the beginning of the quarter if you're going to hit your $10 million quota at the end of the quarter. By effectively managing your pipeline with enough lead time, you can crack the whip and increase the amount of activity that's necessary from your sales force.

☞ MANAGE THE CUSTOMER BASE

There's nothing wrong with your sales force maintaining a strong relationship with your customers—especially if those customers are prospects for new or additional business. However, a good sales manager needs to maintain as strong or even a stronger relationship than the sales professional with key customers. You never want to be held hostage by a weak salesperson because of the strong relationship with a customer that you don't have. Nor do you want to be in a position of trying to establish a relationship with your customers if your salesperson leaves you. Obviously, if one of my salespeople leaves to work for the competition, as long as I have maintained a strong relationship with the customer base, I may have lost a salesperson but I will be able to retain my clients.

> *Experience is not what happens to you; it's what you do with what happens to you.*
>
> — Aldous Huxley

CHAPTER 24
Lead By Example

*Leadership is the art of getting someone else to do
something you want done because he wants to do it.*
— Dwight D. Eisenhower

As the leader or manager of the sales force, your words should be the gospel and your actions must be the stone into which the words are carved. Too often words can be hollow without action. True leadership and motivation are produced by example. It will always be your actions and your behavior that create respect from the people you manage.

☞ LIFE PLANS

Naturally, you will have sales goals or quotas for your salespeople to reach. These goals represent company objectives—numbers which have been derived by the hierarchy of the company, numbers which will reflect the projected profit your company wants to earn, and numbers which will be pleasing to the Board of Directors and the shareholders of the company. Therefore, wouldn't it seem that these numbers are important to everyone?

Often, the corporate numbers have no meaning to an individual sales professional. I'm not suggesting that any or all sales professionals aren't team players; however, if the corporate numbers do not reflect personal meaning in a sales professional's life, the salesperson and the corporation are out of sync and not walking in step together.

If the quota you place on a salesperson represents income which is above that salesperson's comfort zone, it's a simple rule of human nature that he or she most likely will not reach that quota. He or she will have set the bar much lower and will have already reached those numbers before reaching yours. Conversely, if the quota you place on a salesperson is below his or her comfort zone, in all probability the salesperson will surpass your numbers on the way to achieving his or her own.

One of the most powerful and motivating things you can do with the salespeople you manage is to help them build a life plan. Take the time to work with each one of them to clarify and uncover what they would really like to achieve in life. Remember, a life plan is based on their dreams and desires—the lifestyle they wish to have, the things they want to do, and the accomplishments they wish to achieve for themselves and their family. Only after all of this has been laid out and put into a plan with a timeline can money or quotas have meaning. Life plans are really not about money; however, the plans must be funded. In most cases, the funds necessary to support a life plan require that the salesperson surpass your quota as a by-product of funding his or her life plan.

☞ YOUR MANDATE NEEDS TO BE REFLECTED IN THE COMP PLAN

Generally, every manager and corporation have subtle sales objectives that they would like to achieve. For instance, let's assume a corporation has developed a new product they would like to promote; however, the sales force may be uncomfortable with the new product, or may not place any greater emphasis on selling the new product over existing items in their line. In cases like this, it's important that your mandate is reflected in the salesperson's compensation plan.

Let's pretend your salespeople earn 5% commission on products. To achieve your mandate, the commission on sales of the new product should be set at 10%. The issue could be a new product, new accounts, or whatever. The best way to achieve your team's strategy is for each individual salesperson to benefit from the team goal.

> *In matters of style, swim with the currents . . . in*
> *matters of principle, stand like a rock.*
> — Thomas Jefferson

☞ WORK ETHIC

There is no greater way to lead by example than to have a stronger work ethic than anyone you manage. The harder you work, the harder your team will work. The longer you work, the longer your team will work. The best way to get additional effort from the people you manage is by allowing them to see you exert additional effort.

Managers who watch the clock and leave the office at 5:00 PM on the nose will instill that same pattern in their employees. The term "corporate culture" is a cliché. In most organizations, the culture is usually a result of what the boss is doing. Be extremely conscious of the trouble line (Chapter 5)—the 8:00 to 5:00 time frame when prime sales activity will take place. If your team witnesses that you spend a high percentage of time above the trouble line, they will feel compelled to follow suit.

☞ SENSE OF URGENCY

A sense of urgency goes hand-in-hand with work ethic. If you have it, you will instill it in others. Time is the one thing we have all been given in equal amounts. Time is also the one thing we can never recapture. You can't tell your people to have a sense of urgency. They will only develop one if you have one. Lead by example and show them how much value you place on time. This will not only encourage them to be prompt for meetings and to turn in reports when they are due; it will also, subconsciously, help them speed up their selling cycle.

The most important quality in a leader is that of being acknowledged as such. All leaders whose fitness is questioned are clearly lacking in force.
— Andre Maurois

CHAPTER 25

Make Friends Away From Work

Life consists not in holding good cards but in playing those you hold well.

— Josh Billings

Often sales managers are promoted from within. They spent their time on the battlefield, made a name for themselves as a successful salesperson and earned the right to take a step up the ladder into sales management. This progression has its benefits. It usually builds morale in the department or within the company by showing that hard work pays off. Also, the transition usually benefits the company, since the individual is familiar with the company.

There is a downside though. It's possible for other members of the team to resent the individual who was promoted or to be jealous of that person's success. Also, since the sales manager came from the rank and file, on a personal level, he may be friends with people he now has to manage.

In my twenty-five-year business and sales career, I think I've seen every bad situation that is possible. As a result, I am a true believer that this should be a hard and fast rule: *Never hire your buddies.*

Any time you are promoted from within and you now have to manage people who may be your friends or who you may have a social relationship with outside of work, you need to establish firm, upfront ground rules. Sit down with your friend who you are now managing and say, "Joe, I value our friendship and I certainly hope that my new position never jeopardizes that friendship. I want to give you a head's up so we can avoid any bad situations. I'm going to have to be tougher on you than anyone else. I'm going to expect more from you than anyone else. If the rest of the management team or sales force ever thought that you were professionally benefiting from our friendship, it would be bad for both of us. So, I'm going to need to go over-board to prove to management and the sales force that you're not being given preferential treatment."

By establishing these ground rules, hopefully, you can keep Joe from trying to take advantage of you. When it comes time to "lay down the law," it will be much easier to do.

☞ IS THIS AS GOOD AS IT GETS?

Any time you are displeased with the performance of one of your sales-people, or you're on the verge of firing one of your salespeople, you need to have an "Is this as good as it gets" conversation or meeting with them. Use this exact verbiage. For example: "Beth, for the past several months, your numbers have been down and your attitude has been questionable. I need to know one thing. Is this as good as it's going to get?"

Beth is either going to tell you, "No. I can and will do better." Then, you establish expectations for the two of you. Or, she will tell you, "Yes. This is as good as it's going to get." Which now puts you in a perfect position to deal with the situation.

Rather than lecturing or criticizing your salespeople's performance, get in the habit of asking them, "Is this as good as it's going to get?" If the sales-person says the situation is as good as it's going to get, you will then have to make a decision. Can you live with the salesperson and their current perfor-mance and/or attitude? Or, is it time to part company?

☞ FUNGUS ELIMINATION

There is nothing worse than a fungus in a sales force, because it grows and it spreads. The fungus reproduces and multiplies. When you manage salespeople, you must eliminate any and all fungus the minute you're con-vinced it is a fungus. No. A fungus is not an issue. A fungus is a salesperson. I'm not just talking about your worst performer. The fungus could be your best performer.

A fungus is a salesperson who has a bad attitude, loves to complain, loves to point fingers and is a rebel without a cause. Worst of all, they try to recruit others to their cause. The fungus wants other people on the sales force to be as disgruntled as they are. If you don't eliminate them, over time, they'll tear your sales force apart.

The only way you can live with a fungus is if they're a good producer and they're completely isolated from the rest of the sales force. However, even salespeople who work in remote offices or territories are rarely isolated from the rest of the sales force.

Let's assume you have a sales force of ten people. Nine people may have a good attitude and a good outlook, and one person is a fungus. It only makes sense that the power of nine might cure the fungus and the one person's attitude will come around. It never works that way. It's always the opposite. The one fungus will spread and infect some of the other nine.

Make fungus elimination part of your management strategy.

☞ ACTIVELY INTERVIEW

Don't just interview when you have an opening. Make recruiting and interviewing a weekly activity. The more actively you interview, the more your sales force will stay on its toes. Actively interviewing also puts you in a position that when an opening suddenly occurs, you can fill it promptly. Even if turnover is not a large issue for you, and your sales force is relatively stable, you should consider purging the bottom 10% on an annual basis. A sales force is very similar to a chain—it's only as strong as its weakest link. If you actively interview, you're always in a position to get rid of your weakest link.

If you actively interview, the worst thing that can happen is you might find someone who is better than your worst salesperson.

Use this simple method to evaluate your sales force at least once a quarter.

SKILLS VS. ATTITUDE & COMMITMENT

High Skills / Low A & C	High Skills / High A & C
Low Skills / Low A & C	Low Skills / High A & C

Evaluate every person on your sales force in the following manner. Rate them from one to ten on his or her attitude and commitment—one through five is low, six through ten is high. Now also rate each on his or her skill level as a sales professional. After rating every salesperson, each person will fall into one of the four boxes.

High Skills / Low Attitude and Commitment—Salespeople who fall into this category could possibly be a fungus. Keep your eye on them.

High Skills / High Attitude and Commitment—These are your heroes and, most likely, your best producers.

Low Skills / Low Attitude and Commitment—You should have fired these people yesterday. Don't wait any longer.

Low Skills / High Attitude and Commitment—These are the people you need to spend your time managing and invest training dollars in.

> *The way up and the way down are one and the same.*
>
> — Heraclitus

SUMMARY OF PART FOUR
Sales Manager's Handbook: Six Principles of Sales Management

It's almost impossible for a sales manager to have a script or a formatted outline of his daily activities. Sales management involves rolling with the punches, thinking and acting on your feet, and of course, putting out fires. It is important though to have basic principles which you follow in order to guide you through your management decisions and endeavors.

To build and maintain an effective sales force, you must begin with the right raw materials (people). Effective hiring and training criteria certainly makes the job of managing much easier. Never reduce your standards in order to accommodate your sales force. Rather, always be raising the bar.

Six Principles of Sales Management

1. Find and Interview the Right Candidates
2. Evaluate and Hire Candidates Correctly
3. Manage—Don't Babysit
4. Stop Rescuing Your Salespeople
5. Lead By Example
6. Make Friends Away From Work

GLOSSARY:

Sales Terms and Tactics

SALES TERMINOLOGY

Above-the-Line Habit—Daily sales activities that directly lead to a sale.

Accident Report—Analysis of your selling strategy to determine what went wrong.

Amiable—One of four styles, or personality types, that can predict a person's thought processes and actions.

Analytical—One of four styles, or personality types, that can predict a person's thought processes and actions.

Appraisal—The third stage of the buying cycle.

Awakening—The first stage of the buying cycle

Baggage—Obstacles and problems created by salespeople in their own minds.

Bending Over—Giving a concession to a prospect without getting something in return.

Bonding & Rapport—Establishing trust and comfort with a prospect.

Bravery—Doing what must be done, even when you don't feel like doing it.

Buying Cycle—Stages which corporations or individuals go through when making purchasing decisions.

Champion, The—The most influential person in a corporate buying situation.

Comfort Zone—Boundaries we establish in which to live and operate.

Commitment—Doing whatever it takes to become successful.

Compass—The most basic sales activities necessary on a daily basis in order to reach your goals.

Compelling Reason—The number one factor of why someone will do business with you or buy your product or service.

Contact Management System—Organizational tool to keep track of people, dates, times and activities.

Corporate Food Chain—The hierarchy of title and influence within a corporation.

Daily Journal Habit—A daily five to ten minute exercise used to recap the day and plan tomorrow.

Decision Matrix—An organized and systematic series of questions used to determine a prospect's decision-making criteria.

Decision Zone—The third step in your selling strategy.

Denial—Not facing or coming to grips with the reality of a situation.

Desire—A passion for success.

Destination—Goals.

Dreams—Achievement or goals without a plan.

Driver—One of four styles, or personality types, that can predict a person's thought processes and actions.

Due Diligence—The second stage of the buying cycle.

End Zone—The last step in your selling strategy.

Evaluations—Tests or measurement tools to determine the strengths or weaknesses of sales candidates.

Farmer—A salesperson who is comfortable working existing accounts and is not proficient at developing new accounts.

Fear of Failure—Not beginning a process which may have a negative outcome.

Fungus—A salesperson with a bad attitude which may be contagious to others.

Goals—A dream with a plan. A destination.

Head Trash—Obstacles and problems created by salespeople in their own minds.

Huddle, The—Corporate maneuvering during the buying cycle.

Hunter—A salesperson who is proficient at prospect for new accounts.

Insanity—Doing the same thing over and over again and expecting a different result.

Just Do It Habit—Taking immediate action. The opposite of procrastination.

Landmines—Stalls, objections and issues which can derail the sales process.

Life Plan—Goals you wish to achieve in your lifetime with a method and strategy to achieve them.

Life Scripting—Values and thought processes developed in our early childhood.

Middle of the Pack Syndrome—Companies operating in a market space in which they are neither the best product or the cheapest product.

Mirror and Match—Emulating your prospect's body language and tonality.

Money Zone—The second step in your selling strategy.

Need for Approval—A salesperson's desire to be accepted and liked by his prospect.

Negotiating—Giving something up for something else in return.

Negotiating with Yourself—Landmines and obstacles salespeople mentally create for themselves.

Primary Learning Sense±—Learning and decision mechanism an individual is most comfortable with.

Problem Zone—The first step of your selling strategy.

Roadmap—Strategic plan to achieve your goals.

Role Separation—Detaching your personal emotions from the role you are playing (career; salesperson).

Selling—Getting your price for your products or services under your terms and conditions.

Selling Strategy—A systematic plan or method used when working your selling cycle.

Social Being—One of four styles, or personality types, that can predict a person's thought processes and actions.

Solution Zone—The fourth step in your selling strategy.

Super Consumer—Someone who invests extraordinary time and effort in shopping for the best prices and terms.

Thirty-Second Commercial—Determined and rehearsed script to be used via the telephone to help a sales professional set up sales appointments.

Trouble Line—8:00 a.m. – 5:00 p.m. Monday through Friday. Business hours.

Uncomfortable Discussing Money—Self-explanatory.

Winner/Loser Profile—A graph or matrix used to help discover the common components of winning deals vs. losing deals.

NEGOTIATION TACTICS

The Flinch—This is conveyed through body language or a look of disbelief on your face when asked for a concession.

The Take Away—This is when you imply that you want to revisit and possibly take away concessions you have already made. The purpose of this tactic is to stop the prospect from continuing to ask for more.

Offer Options—Let's assume there are five issues on which negotiations are still taking place. Tell your prospect you can concede on two or maybe three of these issues but you have to hold firm on the others. Give them a choice on the two or three they want.

Higher Authority—Defer to higher authority. You cannot give them what they are asking for because it is not within your power and you will never get approval.

Let's Pretend—Use the verbiage, "Let's pretend, I conceded on this issue" and ask . . . what happens next? If what happens next is to your advantage, or helps finalize the deal, then you might think about conceding the point. However, if it does not move you closer, then why concede? And, tell your prospect that.

The End of the World As We Know It—This tactic involves taking your prospect to the edge of some terrible outcome and showing them you have the strength to walk away. Usually, both parties—not just the seller—have a great deal to lose if the negotiations fail in the fourth stage of the buying cycle.

Truth Detector—The use of flattery or humor in the negotiating process at the right time, or at critical times, can help you uncover how firm the prospect is on an issue and where the line can really be drawn.

Standard Practice—When your prospect is negotiating with you and asks for certain concessions, get used to using the terminology back to them, "This is not standard practice." This will begin to wear on them. Very few people enjoy constantly breaking the law.

Home Field Advantage—In the final stage of the buying cycle, when negotiations are taking place, try to get the prospect to make a road trip to your office or facility. This tells you how committed they are to getting the deal done, which is to your advantage. It also, subconsciously, reinforces their commitment.

Never Be Outnumbered—Negotiate one-on-one or two-on-two. Try never to be caught in a situation where there are more of them than there are of you. If you ever find yourself outnumbered, always use the tactics "higher authority" and "this is not standard procedure."

SALES TACTICS

Sales Tactic # 1: Mutual Agreement—A mutual agreement is when you get your prospect to agree to something at some future point in time.

Sales Tactic # 2: OK not OK—This is when a sales professional acts a little unsure of themselves and may be perceived to be a bit un-confident which results in the prospect feeling more comfortable and self-assured.

Sales Tactic # 3: Rotation—Rotation is when your prospect asks you a question, you ignore their question and don't answer it. Rather, you respond to them by asking them a question.

Sales Tactic # 4: Tentative Maneuvering—This is the art of phrasing questions, statements, responses or opinions in more of a tentative manner than a positive manner.

Sales Tactic # 5: Future to Present—This tactic is when you take your prospect into the future (so they have a vision of the future), then bring them back to the present.

Sales Tactic # 6: The One-Liner—A statement or question that rolls out of your mouth to keep you from talking to yourself and puts the ball back in their court for further explanation.